HONEY

HONEY

NATURE'S WONDER INGREDIENT: 100 AMAZING USES FROM TRADITIONAL
CURES TO FOOD AND BEAUTY, WITH TIPS, HINTS AND 40 TEMPTING RECIPES

JENNI FLEETWOOD

with photographs by Michelle Garrett

LORENZ BOOKS

This edition is published by Lorenz Books,
an imprint of Anness Publishing Ltd,
Hermes House,
88–89 Blackfriars Road,
London SE1 8HA
tel. 020 7401 2077
fax 020 7633 9499

www.lorenzbooks.com
www.annesspublishing.com

If you like the images in this book
and would like to investigate using
them for publishing, promotions or
advertising, please visit our website
www.practicalpictures.com for
more information.

UK agent: The Manning Partnership Ltd;
tel. 01225 478444; fax 01225 478440;
sales@manning-partnership.co.uk

UK distributor: Grantham Book Services Ltd;
tel. 01476 541080; fax 01476 541061;
orders@gbs.tbs-ltd.co.uk

North American agent/distributor:
National Book Network; tel. 301 459 3366;
fax 301 429 5746; www.nbnbooks.com

Australian agent/distributor:
Pan Macmillan Australia;
tel. 1300 135 113; fax 1300 135 103;
customer.service@macmillan.com.au

New Zealand agent/distributor:
David Bateman Ltd; tel. (09) 415 7664;
fax (09) 415 8892

Publisher: Joanna Lorenz
Project Editor: Anne Hildyard
Photography and styling: Michelle Garrett
Designer: Sarah Rock
Contributing Author: Wendy Kavanagh
Production Controller: Wendy Lawson

Ethical Trading Policy:
At Anness Publishing we believe that
business should be conducted in an ethical
and ecologically sustainable way, with
respect for the environment and a proper
regard to the replacement of the natural
resources we employ.

As a publisher, we use a lot of wood pulp
to make high-quality paper for printing,
and that wood commonly comes from
spruce trees. We are therefore currently
growing more than 750,000 trees in three
Scottish forest plantations: Berrymoss
(130 hectares/320 acres), West Touxhill
(125 hectares/305 acres) and Deveron
Forest (75 hectares/185 acres). The forests
we manage contain more than 3.5 times
the number of trees employed each year in
making paper for the books we manufacture.
Because of this ongoing ecological
investment programme, you, as our
customer, can have the pleasure and
reassurance of knowing that a tree is being
cultivated on your behalf to naturally
replace the materials used to make the book
you are holding.
Our forestry programme is run in
accordance with the UK Woodland
Assurance Scheme (UKWAS) and will be
certified by the internationally recognized
Forest Stewardship Council (FSC). The FSC is
a non-government organization dedicated to
promoting responsible management of the
world's forests. Certification ensures forests
are managed in an environmentally
sustainable and socially responsible way. For
further information about this scheme, go to
www.annesspublishing.com/trees

© Anness Publishing Ltd 2008

Notes:
Bracketed terms are intended for
American readers.

For all recipes, quantities are given in both
metric and imperial measures and, where
appropriate, in standard cups and spoons.
Follow one set of measures, but not a mixture,
because they are not interchangeable.

Standard spoon and cup measures are
level. 1 tsp = 5ml, 1 tbsp = 15ml,
1 cup = 250ml/8fl oz.

Australian standard tablespoons are 20ml.
Australian readers should use 3 tsp in place
of 1 tbsp for measuring small quantities of
gelatine, flour, salt, etc.

American pints are 16fl oz/2 cups. American
readers should use 20fl oz/2.5 cups in place
of 1 pint when measuring liquids.

Electric oven temperatures in this book are
for conventional ovens. When using a fan
oven, the temperature will probably need to
be reduced by about 10–20°C/20–40°F.
Since ovens vary, you should check with your
manufacturer's instruction book for guidance.

The nutritional analysis given for each recipe
is calculated per portion (i.e. serving or item),
unless otherwise stated. If the recipe gives a
range, such as Serves 4–6, then the
nutritional analysis will be for the smaller
portion size, i.e. 6 servings. Measurements for
sodium do not include salt added to taste.

Medium (US large) eggs are used unless
otherwise stated.

Publisher's note

While every effort has been made to ensure
accuracy when researching this book, the
information on the therapeutic and
cosmetic value of honey is often anecdotal
and is not intended as a substitute for the
advice of a qualified professional. Any use
to which the recommendations, ideas and
techniques are put is at the reader's sole
discretion and risk.

Honey should not be given to children
under the age of 1 year. In rare instances, it
may contain spores of the bacteria
Clostridium botulinum. Most older children
and adults can cope with this, but because
a baby's digestive system is immature, the
bacteria can multiply in it and cause
problems. If you are pregnant, breastfeeding
or have a medical condition and are unsure
as to whether you should be having honey,
consult your doctor.

The very young, the elderly, pregnant
women and those in ill-health or with a
compromised immune system are advised
against eating dishes containing raw eggs.

Contents

INTRODUCTION

Honey is one of the oldest foods in existence. It has been used for thousands of years in natural remedies and beauty products and in food and drink.

It has been called liquid gold, the golden elixir and the gift of the gods. For centuries, man has harvested honey, revelling in its satisfying sweetness and marvelling at its therapeutic qualities. Globally, honey consumption is at an all-time high, so what better time to examine its benefits and celebrate this remarkable ingredient?

The history of honey is much, much older than mankind. Until recently it was assumed that the bees responsible for this bounty evolved around 60 million years ago. That was until an extraordinary discovery in 2006 – a tiny primitive bee, perfectly preserved in amber, which scientists dated as more than 100 million years old. The find, made in a mine in northern Burma, excited particular interest since the insect had characteristics of both modern bees and wasps, though it favoured the former. This suggests that both types of insect shared a common ancestor.

Above: These bees are perfectly preserved in a resin called amber. They are believed to be more than 100 million years old, confirming that bees originated before humans.

Quite when man first stumbled upon honey is not known. Perhaps it was a lucky discovery made when a hunter climbed a tree to escape a wild beast and came across a hive dripping with honey. However it happened, it was the beginning of a love affair with honey that has lasted centuries.

In ancient cultures honey had a role in weddings, births and funerals and in some countries; such as ancient Greece, honey symbolized fertility, beauty and love. Taxes were paid with honey in ancient Egypt and offered to the gods in the form of

Above: A worker bee gathers pollen and nectar and in the process pollinates the flowers that it visits.

a fermented drink that was called 'the nectar of the gods.' As well as its use in the kitchen in food and drink, honey is prized for its healing properties and it is recognized to have antiseptic and antibacterial properties, which can be exploited in natural remedies for various complaints. Honey has the ability to attract and retain moisture, so has a long tradition of being used in creams and lotions. Another useful domestic by-product from the hive is beeswax, which is used to make polishes, soaps, face creams, good quality candles and, with honey, to make lip balms and bath and beauty products.

Considering the astonishing effort that bees make to produce our honey, it is only fitting that the fruit of their labours should be used for so many benefits – adding unique flavour to food, healing remedies, beauty care and some household uses. And it is a totally pure and natural product.

Above: A honeycomb, sealed with wax, contains liquid honey.
Right: The colour of honey varies depending on the floral source.

ALL ABOUT HONEY

It is known that primitive people collected and ate wild honey as far back as 7000BCE and ever since, humans have been fascinated by everything related to honey. This chapter explores a selection of superstitions and myths that have grown up around honey. It also explains what honey is; how it is collected and has been over the centuries; and how the beekeeper uses his expertise to help to make different types of honey. The useful by-products of the hive – pollen, propolis, royal jelly and beeswax – are also described.

Left: A beehive is set in a garden with a profusion of colourful flowers. Foraging bees are attracted to the plants when gathering nectar.

HONEY LEGENDS AND MYTHS

The magical sweetness of honey and its insect origin has made it the subject of enduring myths and legends. Bees, too, have often been used as symbols of the gods.

For centuries, honey has been surrounded by mystique. To the ancients, it seemed inconceivable that so miraculous a substance could actually be produced by insects. Instead, they reasoned that bees must be messengers of the gods, put on Earth to harvest the sweetness that was supplied by divine forces. Honey fell as rain or dew, or was conveyed to Earth by bees that, being magical themselves, were able to flit between heaven and man's domain.

The ancient Egyptians believed that bees were formed from the teardrops of Ra, the Sun God, and honey was his gift to mankind. At one time, Lower Egypt was called Bee Land and the winged insect was a potent symbol.

The association of honey with sunshine and the dawn is also an ancient Indo-Aryan belief. The *Rig-Veda*, Sanskrit scriptures written more than three thousand years ago, ascribe the daily rising of the sun to the Aswins, children of the Sun and Moon, who ride the heavens in a golden chariot filled with honey. Bees and honey have great significance in this sacred work, and incarnations of the gods are often indicated by the presence of bees in religious pictures, sculptures or carvings.

Classical legends

Greek and Roman gods were often associated with bees and honey. Legend has it that the infant Zeus was saved from death by a diet of milk and honey brought by the nymph Melissa after his mother hid him to prevent his father devouring him. But Melissa's role in the

Above: The Discovery of Honey by Bacchus, *c.1499 (tempera on panel) by Piero di Cosimo (c.1642–1521). The scene was described by Ovid in* The Fasti.

deception was discovered, and she was turned into a worm. When Zeus discovered this he was furious, and immediately transformed Melissa into a queen bee, with more bees as attendants.

Ambrosia, the food of the gods, was based on nectar or honey. Honey was believed to come from paradise, and, like the ancient Egyptians, the Greeks believed it dropped from the skies as dew. The Greek historian Plutarch called honey 'the saliva of the stars'.

Many cultures linked stars with bees and honey. Teutonic tribespeople imagined the stars to be swarms of bees, while the moon was a giant bowl, filled with honey and mead. At night it dripped sweetness on to the Earth.

Honey often features in Norse mythology. Mead, an alcoholic drink made from honey, was regularly drunk by Odin and his henchmen, either from their drinking horns or, after battle, from the skulls of their enemies.

Above: Honey guides feed on bees as they exit the nest, and help people find honey.

African tales

The San people of South Africa and Botswana are often aided in their hunts for wild honey by a honey guide. This is a small bird that likes to feed on bee larvae and beeswax, which it cannot retrieve unaided. The bird therefore enlists the help of either an animal, usually a honey badger, or a human, and attracts attention by making a shrill cry and fluttering until its elected assistant begins to follow. It then heads for the bees' nest, stopping and waiting several times if necessary, until it is certain that it is being followed.

The San always leave a generous portion of honeycomb for the bird, for if they fail to do so, they believe that next time the honey guide appears, it will lead them straight toward a leopard or a venomous snake.

In West Africa and Cuba, honey is associated with the Yoruba goddess of love, Oshun, who is always depicted wearing a yellow dress. Oshun is a water spirit, symbolizing clarity. She is also linked to fertility and childbearing. Women who ask her help bring her offerings of honey, which they first taste to ensure it has not been tampered with by someone who wishes the goddess ill.

Superstitions

Many cultures believe bees to be the souls of the dead. There is a superstition that they must always be informed of important events in the family, especially if there is a death. In parts of the United States, if a beekeeper dies, the new keeper must tell the bees what has happened, and inform them that he is now their master.

Bees must be informed of weddings, too, and should be told if they are about to be moved. If a bee flies into your house, you can expect a visitor, and if the bee circles a sleeping child, the infant will be blessed with good luck and long life. Nobody knows the precise origin of the word honeymoon but it may go back to the days of the ancient Egyptians, when honey was used in marriage rituals. In medieval Europe, newlyweds were given enough mead to last them from one full moon to the next. This may explain how the word came to be used after a wedding. In Anglo-Saxon England, the bride's father supplied the mead, which was believed to enhance fertility.

Above: This picture by Rossetti, c.1850, is of Rene D'Anjou and Jeanne de Laval enjoying their honeymoon. It may be a myth, but it is thought honey was used in marriage rites.

WHAT IS HONEY?

Honey undergoes a complex process in the hive to convert it from nectar to a golden liquid. Moisture is removed, then the honeycomb cells are sealed with wax to protect the honey.

To understand what honey is, it is first necessary to know a little about nectar, a sweet liquid produced by plants to attract female worker bees and other insects to the flowers, and thus assist in the process of pollination. When a bee lands on a flower it is guided to the nectar by a pattern of lines on the petals. These marks, or nectar guides, are difficult for a human to detect, but they are specifically tailored to a bee's vision and act like signposts for bees.

Nectar is a solution of sugars in water, with small amounts of amino acids, vitamins, proteins and enzymes. The precise chemical composition and concentration varies, depending on the type of plant, the soil in which it grows, temperature and humidity levels and moisture in the soil. Bees tend not to mix sources when on a foraging flight, but collect all their nectar from one type of plant. This pattern of behaviour is exploited by beekeepers intent on producing monofloral honeys (from a single source). When the chosen flower comes into bud, they make sure that the supers (boxes above the brood boxes in which the bees store honey) in their hives are completely drained of the last type of honey produced. With their favourite food within reach, the bees will confine themselves to the source selected for them by the beekeeper.

Honeybees

There are around 20,000 species of bees. Most species are solitary, and while they collect nectar and pollen, they do this purely for their own use. Only a few

Above: A little boy looks through the viewing panel in a beehive to check out what is happening inside the hive. This facility helps beekeepers spot any infestations in the hive.

varieties of bees store honey. These include the South American stingless bees and bumblebees. For champion honey production, however, no bee is as efficient as the true honeybee. There are several types of honeybees, including dwarf and giant species. All live in complex colonies, but many are not suitable for containment in hives. The domesticated bee is *Apis mellifera*. Native to Europe, Africa and the Middle East, this type of bee now has a huge range, since it has been introduced into North and South America, and Australia.

Above: This magnified picture shows a honeybee sucking up nectar.

Above: A beekeeper in Utah uses smoke to calm bees before moving the hive.

From nectar to honey

The conversion of nectar to honey begins while the bee is still in flight. Various enzymes are added to the nectar, the most notable of which is invertase. This breaks down sucrose in the nectar into glucose and fructose.

Back at the hive, the bee regurgitates the partially processed nectar and transfers it to waiting worker bees. They work it in their mouths, adding more enzymes before depositing the sap in an empty cell in the brood box.

For the processed nectar to be transformed into honey, about half of its moisture content must be removed. This happens in two ways: by evaporation, due to the heat inside the hive, and by fanning, a process whereby worker bees waft warm air over the cells. As the moisture level decreases and the solution becomes more concentrated, more chemical changes occur in the sap.

When a cell is almost full to the brim, and the moisture content has dropped to 18 per cent, the cells are sealed with wax to prevent further moisture loss and protect the contents.

Composition of honey

The composition of individual types of honey varies considerably. All honey is primarily a highly concentrated sugar solution. The main sugars in honey (about 85 per cent of the solids present) are fructose and glucose, which are both simple sugars, but there will also be small amounts of as many as 22 complex sugars, including sucrose.

In general, there will be slightly more fructose than glucose, making the honey less likely to crystallize. Acacia honey is very resistant to crystallization, due to its high fructose levels. Rapeseed, or canola, honey, in which glucose is dominant, granulates very quickly.

BEES AT RISK

Above: An adult worker bee has been infected by two parasitic mites (Varroa destructor) on its thorax.

For many years beekeepers have worried about dwindling stocks. In the United States alone, it has been estimated that the number of managed bees in hives has declined by up to a quarter. Wild bees are also affected.

The phenomenon is causing great concern, not just because of what it means in terms of honey production, but also because of its effect on the pollination of plants and therefore food stocks.

A number of reasons have been suggested for the decline in bee populations. Most of the blame has been directed at parasites and diseases. Mites such as *Varroa destructor* and *Acarapis woodi* caused major losses in the 1980s and 90s, and foul brood disease has been a widespread problem.

The use of pesticides has killed bees in large numbers. Loss of habitat is another issue. Modern farming methods often devote huge swathes of land to a single crop. When it flowers, there is ample food for the bees, but when the nectar flow is over, they are in serious trouble. Many beekeepers address this problem by moving the hives but this can stress the bees and spread infection.

Colony Collapse Disorder, in which formerly healthy hives are discovered to be almost empty, is a huge concern. Experts are unsure as to the cause of the collapse.

Above: Hives are arranged around fruit trees in Siberia, Russia. Bees and other insects visit the blossoms to gather nectar and to assist in pollination.

BEEKEEPING THROUGH THE AGES

The development of beekeeping took honey from being an occasional treat to a useful source of sweetness that could be easily harvested from tailor-made hives.

Apiculture, or beekeeping, probably began around 3000 to 4000BC. The first beekeepers, as opposed to hunters, simply searched for a hollow tree in which wild bees had made their nest. They cut down the tree, isolated the portion of trunk containing the nest, and carried this home. When it was realized that bees would be equally happy in man-made objects, provided these were dark, dry and defensible, swarms of bees were encouraged to occupy these instead. Some cultures used vertical, hollow pipes made from wood or clay as rudimentary hives; others employed clay or pottery urns or constructed containers from cork or reeds.

Beekeeping in Egypt and Mesopotamia

Inscriptions on Sumerian tablets suggest that they were among the world's first beekeepers, but it was the ancient Egyptians who really developed the craft. Wild swarms were enticed into specially constructed pottery containers, which were then taken back to the temples and given into the care of priests. By 2600BC apiculture was well established and honey was used medicinally, in beauty preparations and for trade, 110 pots of honey being equal in value to an ox or an ass.

The symbol for honey in Egyptian hieroglyphics was a bee, and beekeeping was represented on reliefs in the Temple of the Sun at Abusir. These carvings show honey being transferred from clay hives to containers for storage. The ancient Egyptians also practised

Above: A beekeeper carefully removes honey from a beehive. In the Oman, beehives are not conventional designs, but are often made from stacked, hollow palm tree trunks.

migratory beekeeping, loading the hives on to rafts that were moved along the Nile so that the bees could gather nectar from plants as they came into full flower. When the nectar ceased to flow, in early February, the itinerant beekeepers returned to Cairo and sold their honey in the markets there.

The ancient Egyptians liked to use honey in cooking, especially for honey cakes, and as offerings to the gods. Jars of honey were buried with the pharaohs, to sustain them in the afterlife, a practice that was also common in Mesopotamia (modern day Iraq), where honey was widely used medicinally.

There are many references to honey in the Bible and it is known that ancient Palestine was a good source of wild

honey. In India, too, the use of honey was widespread. It played (and continues to play) an important role in Ayurvedic medicine, a system of healthcare based on Sanskrit texts that are believed to be more than 3000 years old.

Beekeeping in Greece and Rome

From Egypt, beekeeping spread to ancient Greece and Rome. Aristotle, Hippocrates and Dioscorides sang honey's praises, variously recommending it as a wound salve, a cough medicine, an aid to eliminating body lice, and a cure for earache, ulcers and even haemorrhoids. In Greek mythology there are references to honey, which was regarded as the food of the gods. It was the Greeks who first fully appreciated the subtle differences in flavour in honeys from different sources. Savory and marjoram got honourable mention, but in the opinion of the Greeks the finest honey came from thyme, especially thyme growing on the slopes of Mount Hymettus, near Athens. Honey was the only sweetener available in Europe at the time, aside from syrups made from dried fruits, and herbs such as sweet cicely. It was also widely used for making mead, or honey wine.

The ancient Romans valued honey as much as the Greeks. Apicius, a famous gourmand writing in the 1st century BC, extolled its virtues, using honey in more than half of his recipes, including one for roast dormouse (brushed with honey) and another for honey-baked ham. Honey was often mixed with salty ingredients such as anchovies to create sweet-sour sauces. It was also highly valued as a food preservative.

Above: Two modern beehives are set in a garden with a profusion of colourful flowers. Foraging worker bees are attracted to a wide variety of plants when gathering nectar.

Beekeeping in Britain

How and when beekeeping reached the British Isles isn't known precisely. There is evidence that wild bees were exploited from the very earliest times. Traces of honey have been found on Neolithic pottery remains dating from around five thousand years ago, and beekeeping was apparently practised in England long before the Roman invasion. By the 11th century AD, beekeeping was widespread and was so important that the Domesday Book lists the number of hives each land holder possessed. The hives were often made of wicker, and sometimes they were covered with tree bark or clay.

Skeps, or bee baskets, consisted of coils of straw, reed or grass, bound with hazel or willow fronds. Over decades, hives became more sophisticated and beekeepers tried a variety of different sizes and shapes. Some hives had glass windows inserted in the walls so that people could watch the bees inside; some were placed inside sturdier containers for protection; others were raised on stones to make them less accessible to mice and rats.

Beekeeping and the collection and preparation of honey and beeswax, traditionally male pursuits, later became the province of the woman of the house.

Above: These straw skeps or bee baskets look attractive but it is far easier to look after bees in hives, and also removing honey from a skep can be damaging.

By the beginning of the 18th century, domestic beekeeping was so widespread in Britain that alcoves, or bee boles, were built in the outer walls of cottages to hold the skeps and keep them dry, as the Romans had done centuries before. A similar practice was current in Europe, where bees were sometimes kept in specially constructed cavities between the inner and outer walls of houses.

Many domestic beekeepers became highly proficient at taking care of their bees, providing them with access to water (bees need water for temperature and humidity control as well as brood rearing) and planting flowers with successive flowering periods to ensure an ongoing supply of nectar. Those who did not have gardens of their own were sometimes able to place hives temporarily on public land, or on large private estates. Some landowners actively encouraged the practice, even arranging protection for the beekeepers and their stock. This wasn't purely an altruistic act; the temporary lodgers paid for their stake in honey and beeswax.

Bees in the Americas

The European honeybee (*Apis mellifera*) didn't arrive in North America until the 16th century, when Spanish missionaries introduced them to the west Coast. Not long after that, hives were part of the cargo transported to the east Coast by settlers who followed in the wake of the Pilgrim Fathers.

In South America, two native varieties of stingless bee, *Melipona* and *Trigona*, produced honey. Both the Maya and the Aztecs loved its distinctive flavour and appreciated the sweetness honey contributed to cakes, drinks and even some savoury dishes. The Maya even brewed a type of honey beer, which was reputed to be highly alcoholic. Beekeeping was widely practiced and successive rulers exacted tribute in the form of honey from their subjects. To the Inca of Peru, whose civilization was founded on gold, the colour and sweetness of honey appears to have had special significance, and it was used in temple rituals.

Development of the hive

Until the frame hive was developed, early beekeeping was a labour-intensive pursuit with only limited rewards. The bees did their part perfectly, producing honey in whatever containers their keepers chose to provide, but because bees routinely block up holes in the hives with wax and propolis, leaving only bee-width gaps for access, the honeycomb was welded to the walls. The only way to get it out was to shatter the hive, and this inevitably meant the end of the bees as well. The usual practice was to gas the bees with the smoke from burning sulphur, or to dunk the skeps in water until they drowned. The dead bees were then shaken out, the hive was destroyed and the honeycomb retrieved.

Destroying the bees and their skeps was wasteful and, to many beekeepers, upsetting. It would be so much better to construct hives that allowed easy

Above: A fresco of the Italian School c.1400, depicting The Month of June, shows people collecting honey, indicating that beekeeping has been around for centuries.

removal of the honeycomb without harming the bees or distressing them.

The first step to finding a solution came in the early 18th century with the invention of the box hive. The prototype had bars across the top to which the bees could attach their combs. However, the bees also attached the combs to the sides of the boxes, so the exercise was only partially successful.

Later the same century, Huber and Burnens developed the leaf hive, in which a series of frames were hinged together so that they could be opened like the pages of a book. It was not until the invention of the movable frame hive that beekeepers' prayers were finally answered. Petro Prokopovych, a Ukranian beekeeper, is credited with inventing one of the earliest movable frame beehives. His model was improved upon by Lorenzo Langstroth, an American beekeeper who invented the style of hive that is still used today. It consists of a series of wooden boxes or crates, usually made of cedar or pine, which are stacked on top of each other. Each box contains a series of wire frames, usually nine or ten, suspended from bars, rather like files in a filing cabinet, and it is on these frames that the bees build the wax cells they use for rearing their young and storing pollen and honey.

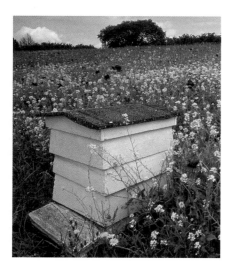

Left: A beehive is set in a flowering meadow to attract bees.

What was clever about the hive Langstroth invented was that he arranged his frames to leave exactly the same gap between the frame and the walls of the hive that a bee would create. The bees built only on the frames, which could now be lifted in and out easily, without disrupting the colony.

A modern hive typically has one or two deep boxes at the base. These are called brood boxes and it is in these that the queen bee lays her thousands of eggs. Shallower boxes, called supers, are stacked as needed on top of the brood boxes for the bees to build honeycombs.

Bees are very self-sufficient. Even the wax they use to build the honeycomb cells is extruded from a gland on their abdomens. However, in order to produce wax, bees need to eat a tremendous amount of honey, so modern beekeepers give the workers a head start by fitting the frames in the brood boxes and supers with sheets of beeswax or plastic imprinted with a honeycomb cell pattern.

Extracting the honey

For centuries, honey was largely eaten as honeycomb, since it was difficult and messy to extract the liquid sealed in the cells. Pressing or crushing the comb resulted in impurities in the honey. Sometimes the honeycomb was heated until the wax dissolved. The resultant mass was put in a bowl until the wax solidified on the surface. When this was lifted off, the liquid honey remained, but by now it had a waxy taste that masked the natural flavours.

This problem was solved when Franz Edler von Hruschka invented the honey extractor. This appliance whirls around the honeycombs, which have been uncapped. Centrifugal force empties the

Above: A beekeeper holds a frame from a modern beehive, on which bees have built wax cells, before taking the honey.

cells and the honey is sprayed on the surface of the drum. It runs down and collects at the bottom of the drum, where there is a tap for drainage.

Honey production today

The major producers of honey include China, Argentina, the United States, Turkey, Ukraine and Mexico; honey is now a global product.

Growing interest in honey's therapeutic and medicinal properties, as well as the public perception of it as a flavoursome natural ingredient, may increase demand further. Honey is a remarkable product, and it will be enjoyed as long as there are bees and beekeepers.

Colony Collapse Disorder

Recently, honey production has been threatened by Colony Collapse Disorder. Some scientists believe that it is a disease and a cure will be found, but if it is an environmental problem, they are less optimistic. Since bees indicate the state of the environment, the best hope is that the problem is a disease.

THE PRODUCTION OF HONEY

Beekeepers manage millions of colonies of bees around the world. Together, they produce 300 million pounds of honey each year, in a variety of forms and flavours.

There are thousands of different types of honey. Since bees will take nectar from any flowering plant, the range is almost infinite. Although honey is produced commercially on a grand scale, it can be hugely rewarding to get to know local beekeepers who can tell you which plants are likely to have provided the nectar for the honey they sell, and who may well offer different types of honey at different stages of the season.

Regulations govern the sale of honey and help to ensure that what is on sale is, as the definition states, a 100 per cent natural product. Honey may not have sugar or starch added to it, and there are strict rules governing colour, blend and composition.

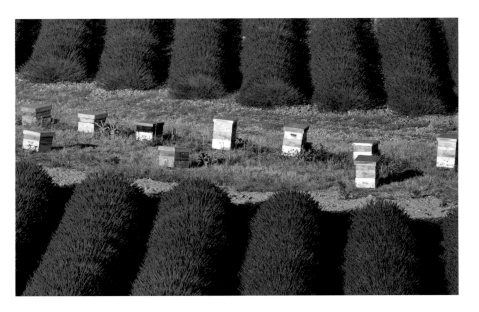

Above: The beautiful violet flowers of lavender attract bees because of their colour and perfume. Nectar from lavender produces honey with a distinctive flavour.

Source of nectar
Most honey is polyfloral, which means that it is made from the nectar of a variety of flowers. Although on each collecting foray a bee will gather nectar from only one type of plant, on subsequent trips she may well visit other flowers, so the honey harvested from the hive will ultimately come from several sources.

However, if there is a local abundance of a particular type of flowering plant which the bees favour, or if bee hives are taken to fields where only one type of plant is cultivated, the chances are that the honey produced will be monofloral, or predominantly from a single source. The third category is blended honey, where different varieties (sometimes from different countries) will be carefully mixed to provide a consistent flavour and colour.

The waggle dance
Scout bees are bees that convey information about a desirable nectar and pollen source to forager bees. This is known as the waggle dance and it is always done on the face of the honeycomb. The display is very distinctive and follows a figure-of-eight pattern. The direction in which the scout

Above: A bee collecting nectar hovers over apple blossom.

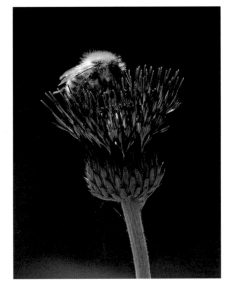

Above: A bee sucks up nectar from clover to produce a popular honey.

bee moves, relative to the position of the sun, gives the foragers information about the route they need to follow. How lively the scout is, and how loudly she buzzes, apparently conveys more detail, such as the distance to the flowers. Finally, the perfume from the pollen she has collected at the site suggests which type of flowering plant is providing the provender for that day.

Colour

Most honey is golden in colour. Hold it up to the light and it looks like bottled sunshine. However, honey can be so pale as to be almost white or so dark as to rival mahogany. The variations depend on the plant source, although some changes in colour can occur during processing or storage. Paler honey sells better than dark honey. However, as consumers become more aware of the many different varieties of honey on the market, darker honeys are becoming more popular. Aside from more pronounced flavours, dark honeys have more antioxidants than pale ones.

In addition to the colours listed above, there have been instances where bees have produced pink, green or even blue honey. Unusual colours are often the result of an accident. Discarded confectionery boxes draw bees, and if the sugar in the box is brightly coloured, the honey will be too. In rare instances, an unusual colour can be a natural phenomenon. In the American state of North Carolina, honey may be blue. Locals attribute this to huckleberries, but no one is sure what causes the effect.

Aroma and flavour

Not all honeys smell the same. Some, especially those based on citrus, have a distinctive scent that intensifies when the honey is warmed. Open a jar of orange blossom honey that has been standing on a breakfast table in the garden on a sunny morning and the perfume will be irresistible. Honey connoisseurs, like professional wine tasters, pay much attention to the 'nose'.

The flavour of honey is determined by the plant nectar from which it came. If the honey is polyfloral, someone with an educated palate may be able to detect the dominant source, at least, but the flavour is not likely to be particularly noteworthy. Where bees forage among mixed plants, as in a wild flower meadow, each batch of honey may be slightly different, depending on the proportions of the various nectars. This is part of the magic if you are buying honey from a small independent producer, but in the commercial world blending will almost certainly have ironed out these subtle differences.

Like the colour, the flavour of honey varies enormously. It can be bland,

Above: Despite the belief that honey is golden in colour, there are numerous shades of honey; these are just three examples of different hues.

subtle, scented, sweet, bitter – even brash. At honey tastings, individuals are blindfolded and then invited to try a selection of honeys. Most novices are amazed to discover how much the flavours vary. Some honeys make an immediate impact. Others are more subtle, but with flavours that develop in the mouth. One or two varieties have a definite aftertaste. There are hundreds of types of honey to choose from, sourced from many different countries, and what one person likes, another may loathe. People who don't like honey may not have tasted enough varieties.

Consistency

Honey can be naturally thin or thick. The moisture content varies a lot. Some types seldom crystallize; others solidify so rapidly that the honey is extremely difficult to extract. A few honeys are thixotropic, which means that they are gel-like in the jar but liquefy if shaken. For many people, texture – the way the honey feels in the mouth – is an important part of the tasting experience.

LOCATION

Honey is produced in countries all over the world, from Siberia to the tip of South America. In many countries, the demand for honey outstrips local supply, so that supplies have to be imported. Of the many factors affecting honey production, weather is paramount. Where the climate is hot all year round, as in equatorial regions, the production of honey is more or less continuous. In colder climates, if the temperature drops too much the bees will die.

POLLEN, PROPOLIS AND ROYAL JELLY

Honey is not the only valuable product produced by bees. Pollen, propolis and royal jelly are used for food or building purposes in the hive, and they are used therapeutically by humans.

Pollen

In addition to collecting nectar to turn into honey, bees forage for pollen, mixing it with saliva and nectar and bringing it back to the hive in the form of neat pellets, which they pack in 'pollen baskets' on their hind legs. The pellets are deposited in storage cells and turned into 'bee bread' by worker bees or collected by the beekeeper; the bees squeeze through a small gap in the hive and the pollen is scraped off their legs as they enter. After the first three days of life, the larvae of all bees other than the queen are fed on this nutritious compound. Pollen is sometimes used as a food supplement, but there are some questions over its efficacy. Side effects have been reported.

Propolis

Bees make propolis, which is incredibly sticky, from resins, saps and other substances that they gather from trees and plants. It is basically a mixture of resin, balm and wax, with essential oils, pollen, organic substances and minerals.

There's rather more evidence of the positive effects of propolis than there is for bee pollen. Propolis is the cement-like substance bees use both when building – to fill holes, reinforce combs and repair damaged cells – and as a disinfectant. The word propolis was allegedly coined by Aristotle. It means 'on behalf of the city' and Aristotle felt it was an apt description of a substance that has many uses in strengthening the hive and keeping it hygienic. A hive

HONEYDEW

Not all honey comes from nectar. A small proportion is made from honeydew, a liquid that is secreted by aphids and other similar insects. This syrupy substance has a sweet taste, like nectar, and bees will sometimes harvest it. Honeydew honey is similar to nectar honey but doesn't contain pollen. In some parts of the world, honeydew honey is highly valued, but some claim that it is often contaminated with environmental pollutants and mould spores.

containing upwards of 50,000 bees in temperatures of around 35°C/95°F and 90 per cent humidity would seem to be the ideal breeding ground for bacteria, yet because bees polish every surface with propolis, infection occurs much less frequently than one might expect.

Above: This artificially coloured electron micrograph of pollen grains shows the sculpted surfaces that allow them to catch the wind and pollinate a female flower.

Above: Pollen grains, which are gathered at the entrance to the beehive.

Propolis is also used to line cells before the queen lays her eggs, again creating a sterile environment.

It is claimed that propolis can alleviate painful joints, treat eczema, relieve respiratory conditions, heal wounds and burns and treat gastro-intestinal problems. It also stimulates the immune system. Many beekeepers simply scrape it off the interior of their hives and take a little every day in alcohol. Health food shops sell propolis in tablet form or as a liquid or spray. Diluted in warm water and used as a gargle, it is said to offer protection against colds and flu. Propolis is also used medicinally to combat gingivitis. Some studies into propolis and royal jelly have suggested that these products may have some value in restricting the growth of certain malignant tumours, but the research is still in its infancy.

Above: Clear honeys in different colours and beautifully constructed honeycomb are the fruits of the bees' labour. One jar of honey is made of nectar from millions of flowers.

Royal jelly

Quite why a diet of royal jelly turns a regular bee grub into a queen is not fully understood. This creamy substance, produced in the hypopharyngeal glands of worker bees, is fed to all larvae for a few days when they first hatch.

When a hive needs a new queen, several larvae are chosen. Instead of being weaned on to bee bread, they are initially fed royal jelly, then they will eat honey and pollen. One of these larvae will become the new queen and she will continue to dine only on royal jelly for the rest of her life. The queen can choose whether or not to fertilize the egg she lays; drones (male bees that have no sting and do not collect nectar) come from unfertilized eggs, while the females such as worker bees and queens come from fertilized eggs. Queens live for years, unlike worker bees and drones, whose lifespans are counted in weeks.

Young workers feed the larvae, clean the hive and produce royal jelly until the glands fail and they then start to build the honeycomb. They then leave the hive and work as a forager.

The link between longevity of the queeen bee and royal jelly has led to the latter being endowed with mystical qualities. Extravagant claims are made for royal jelly but these appear to have little foundation in fact.

Above: Pollen (left) and propolis (right) are both used as food supplements.

Above: Propolis is available in health food shops in capsule form.

Above: The orange-yellow pollen baskets can be clearly seen on the bee's legs.

HONEYCOMBS AND BEESWAX

Beeswax honeycombs are wonderful feats of engineering. The perfectly formed hexagons are the strongest and smallest possible shapes in which to store the maximum amount of honey.

Although everyone is familiar with honey, another product that the industrious bee makes is the lesser known, but no less useful, beeswax. The production of beeswax is essential to the bee colony. They raise their young in the wax comb and use it as storage for surplus honey for the winter.

Beeswax is produced by young worker bees after they have eaten large quantities of honey or sugar syrup. The bees gather together, which raises their temperature and they begin to 'sweat.' The heat that is generated stimulates the production of beeswax, which is formed by wax-producing glands as small, thin scales or flakes on the underside of the bees' abdomen. Other worker bees gather the wax scales and use it to make sheets of hexagonal shaped cells or they transfer the wax scales to the part of the hive that needs some new wax to repair damaged cells.

Beeswax in the hive

There is a very low yield of beeswax. Young worker bees that are between 12 and 17 days old produce the beeswax. What is remarkable is that bees need to eat ten parts of honey to produce one part of beeswax, and it is estimated that bees must fly around 150,000 miles (530,000 kilometres) to produce just one pound (450g) of beeswax. Additionally, the size of the wax glands depends on the age of the worker bee.

Above: Soap made from beeswax has good moisturizing qualities.

The wax glands eventually start to atrophy after the worker bee has made many daily flights.

Beekeepers regularly remove wax from the hive; this encourages the bees to build new wax combs. The wax that is produced is at first white, but owing to the influence of pollen and propolis, it gradually changes to a yellow or brown colour. It is perfectly safe to eat, as are the cappings with which the bees seal the honey cells. Wax that has been used for rearing the new brood is usually dirty and contaminated and is discarded. The wax in which the bees store the honey is fairly clean and can be melted down, filtered and sold.

Temperature control

Beeswax has to be at just the right temperature to allow the bees to mould it into the correct shape. If the temperature is too low, the beeswax

Above: Beeswax candles that are made from 100 per cent beeswax burn efficiently and completely. They do not smoke or drip, and have a pleasant aroma.

will be too brittle and will break up. If the temperature is too high, it will melt. To ensure that they can manipulate the beeswax, the hive is maintained at a temperature of 35°C/95°F.

Varied uses of beeswax

One of the main uses of beeswax is in making high-quality candles, which are used in the home and in churches because they burn hotter, brighter and cleaner than commercial candles. In skin-care products, beeswax has proved to be a superior barrier cream. Its emollient qualities are also recognized in soap making. Some cheeses even have a beeswax coating, which protects the cheese as it ages and does not impart odd flavours.

TIPS FOR MELTING BEESWAX

When melting beeswax, the safest way is to use a bain marie – a small saucepan containing the wax that sits inside a larger pan of water. The wax should not be melted in a pan that is directly over a heat source, such as an electric ring or gas flame, since this can damage the beeswax and if it ignites accidentally, it will burn fiercely. Beeswax gets hotter and hotter until it ignites so it should not be close to a heat source.

The best containers in which to melt beeswax are stainless steel or plated pans. Metals such as copper, brass or iron impart colour to the wax and cause it to look dull. Be cautious when you are pouring out hot beeswax as it has the potential to cause serious burns.

Above: Beeswax is available in many forms: there are blocks, cakes and pellets, which are quicker to melt down when making soaps and candles.

Above: Beeswax pellets are useful when small quantities of wax are required.

Above: A close up of the six-sided cylinders that make up honeycomb.

DIFFERENT FORMS OF HONEY

There are lots of different ways in which honey is sold. You can choose from fresh honeycomb, cut comb, raw honey, heat-treated honey, set honey or organic honey.

Honeycomb

This is the bees' own packaging system. If offered for sale it must be fresh from the hive, and may not contain any eggs or larvae. Before the advent of the honey extraction machine, this is how most people enjoyed honey, but today it is quite difficult to obtain. Biting into the comb (which is edible) breaks the bees' seals on the honeycomb cells and lets the honey flow into your mouth.

Cut comb or chunk honey

This is liquid honey with pieces of honeycomb added to the jar. Acacia honey, which is mild and light, is often used as the base. Acacia honey remains liquid, showing off the honeycomb.

Raw honey

The natural product that has been drained from a honeycomb after the wax covering on the cells has been removed is called raw honey. It will contain some pollen and wax particles. If pressure is applied in the process it will be described as pressed honey. In commercial terms, honey labelled as raw may only have been subjected to minimum processing and low heat.

Liquid honey

This is the most popular form of honey, and the most versatile. When honey is extracted from the comb, it naturally retains some particles of wax, along with propolis and pollen grains. There is a ready market for the natural product, especially if the honey is to be used medicinally. However, these substances give the honey a slightly cloudy appearance. To counter this, beekeepers filter honey through fine mesh, which removes the wax and propolis but leaves the protein-rich pollen behind. It sells in health food shops and at farmers' markets.

Pasteurized or heat-treated honey

In health and hygiene terms, there is no reason why honey should be pasteurized. Its high sugar content protects against the growth of bacteria, and spores of *Clostridium botulinum*, the bacteria that can spell danger for babies, are not destroyed by heat. Pasteurization is carried out largely to satisfy the requirements of industry, since the honey is then less likely to granulate or ferment even if storage conditions are less than perfect. Supermarkets require packagers to produce a clear product. To achieve this, the honey is heated, then put through a rigorous filtration process. Heating dissolves the 'seed crystals' in the honey so it is less likely to granulate.

Set honey

This term can be applied to any honey that has solidified through crystallization of the sugars it contains. This natural process happens faster in some types of honey than in others, usually when there is a high proportion of glucose. Honey that has crystallized spontaneously is grainy, even gritty, and is difficult to get out of the jar, but it can be liquified if it is warmed gently. Do not let it get too hot, or nutrients will be destroyed.

Creamed honey

Also described as whipped, churned, spun honey or honey fondant, this is honey that has been deliberately crystallized in controlled conditions so

Left: Creamed honey is also varied in colour depending on the floral source.

that it forms a smooth mixture. Honey that is high in glucose and will crystallize readily is ideal for creaming. Clover, sunflower and Tasmanian leatherwood are typical examples. The honey is heated, filtered, cooled and chilled. The honey blender 'seeds' the fresh honey with an already crystalline honey of the same type. There is a real art to the operation, since the honey crystals must be kept small and uniform. The mixture is churned, then bottled. At this stage the honey is creamy, setting to a spreading consistency in the jar.

Organic honey

This is subject to strict guidelines. The beehives must be on land that has been certified as organic. Radiating out from the hives, for 6 kilometers/4 miles in any direction, all sources of nectar must be organic crops or untreated wild flowers. The zone may not contain motorways, urban centres, waste dumps or other potential sources of contaminants. Look for a certified product with a label on the jars, stating that the honey comes from approved organic areas.

Honey sticks

These are sold as sweet treats. Slim plastic tubes are filled with pure honey to provide a handy snack or sweetener for tea or coffee.

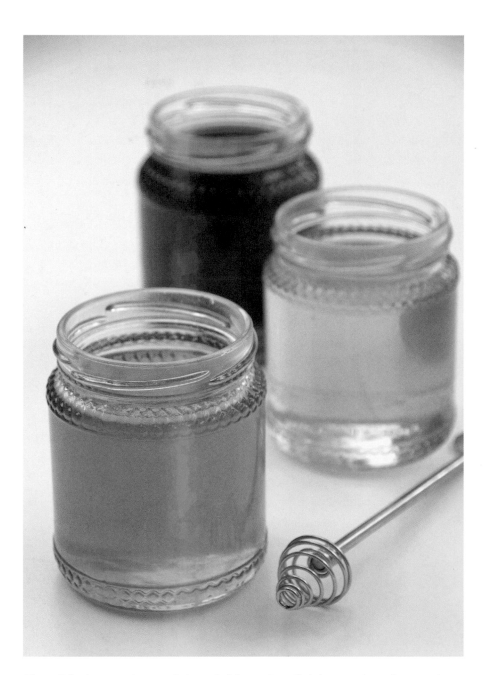

Above: Whether you choose a light or dark honey is really is just a matter of personal preference. Some dark honeys may have a more assertive flavour.

Above: Two different types of honey: clear honey and honeycomb.

Above: Creamed honey has been whipped to produce a smooth, thick mixture.

Above: A wooden honey spoon helps to obtain the honey without dripping it.

POPULAR HONEYS

Honey comes in so many textures and flavours that it can be difficult to choose between them. Make the most of tasting opportunities to try something new.

There are many different types of honey on the market, yet most of us seldom search out the specific. We may prefer our honey set or clear, but that's often as far as choosing a honey goes. Others are more particular, and wouldn't dream of simply picking up the first jar they find on the shelf. Although the differences are more subtle, honey is just as varied as jam, so it is well worth experimenting.

Some honey is labelled by the country of origin. Mexican honey, for instance, is a medium-bodied polyfloral honey from the Yucatan region. It has a rich, fruity flavour and strong floral scent. Australian honey, largely from eucalyptus, has a definite toffee flavour with a hint of raisin. It comes mainly from south-eastern Australia, especially Victoria and New South Wales.

Caribbean honey, another polyfloral, has a rich amber colour and robust, fruity flavour that goes well with rum. Chilean honey typically has a fruity flavour with a hint of vanilla. Honey that is simply labelled 'English' will often be based on nectar from wild flowers and hedgerow blossoms. One of the most popular varieties is a creamed honey with a fudge-like flavour. English beekeeper's honey is direct from the hive and has not been processed commercially. Zambian forest honey has excited interest. This creamy, delectable honey comes from bark hives that are hung in the Miombo forests in the north-west of the country.

There are no specific rules requiring the country of origin to be listed on honey labels, but if an indication is given, the honey must originate wholly from that country. If honey is a blend from various geographical sources, the label should make that clear.

The list that follows is intended to introduce the most popular or typical honeys, plus some rarer types. Most are ascribed to a particular plant, although in reality they are all described as monoflorals; that is, the source is the nectar from the blossoms of that single plant, which is then made into honey. The pictures on these pages show a wide range of honeys from different countries, not all of which have text entries.

Acacia honey

This pale yellow honey has a mild, sweet, floral flavour with hints of vanilla. It actually comes from nectar from the false acacia tree, *Robinia pseudoacacia*. Native to the United States, where it is known as the black locust tree, *Robinia pseudoacacia* is widely cultivated in Hungary, Bulgaria, Romania, France and Italy. Slow to crystallize, as a result of its high fructose levels, acacia honey remains liquid for long periods. It is a good honey for cooking, as it mixes easily in liquids, such as drinks or batters. Cut honeycomb is often placed in jars of acacia honey, since its clarity and pale colour allow the comb to be seen to advantage. It is often blended with other types of honey.

Alfalfa honey

Popular in parts of the United States, this very pale, almost white honey has a delicate flavour. It is not particularly sweet, and sometimes has a slight spiciness, which makes it a useful ingredient for dressings and sauces.

Australian eucalyptus honey

Australian manuka honey

Chilean ulmo blossom honey

Cotswold clear honey

European acacia honey

English beekeeper's honey

Apple blossom honey

This pale gold honey is produced in the spring. It has a sweet flavour with a hint of apple. Some beekeepers in Kent and the English West Country produce it, either as a monofloral or as a polyfloral with wild flowers. In the United States apple blossom honey comes mainly from states in the north and centre of the country.

Arbutus (strawberry tree) honey

The source of this rare and expensive honey is the strawberry tree, a beautiful evergreen that produces exquisite white flowers in the autumn. Native to south-west Ireland and the Mediterranean, the tree takes its name from the small red fruit that it produces. Arbutus honey is amber in colour, with green and grey tones. It has a pungent aroma and bitter

flavour that is very much an acquired taste. Arbutus honey is valued for its therapeutic qualities.

Avocado honey

California and Israel are the main producers of this dark, velvety honey. It tastes nothing like avocado, but has a flavour reminiscent of molasses.

Blackberry honey

This honey is more common in the United States. The colour ranges from white to pale amber. Although brambles or blackberries grow profusely in the United Kingdom, this type of honey is rare there.

Blueberry honey

Popular in the eastern United States and Canada, blueberry honey is said to smell like lemon leaves. It has a fruity flavour,

which some claim really does remind them of blueberries, and a delicate, buttery aftertaste. The colour is golden to medium amber.

Borage honey

Bees love the pretty blue flowers of this common plant, and their nectar produces a pale, delicately flavoured honey. Borage is widely grown in the United Kingdom and on the South Island of New Zealand. This type of honey is slow to crystallize. New Zealanders like to keep it in the refrigerator, as it sets to a chewy consistency when chilled, rather like toffee.

Buckwheat honey

This honey is very dark purple, almost black in colour. The flavour is equally punchy, and suggests molasses or malt.

French sunflower honey

Greek pine honey

Himalayan wild flower honey

Hungarian acacia honey

New Zealand clover honey

New Zealand thyme honey

There is a pronounced aftertaste. Unprocessed buckwheat honey contains significant amounts of pollen. It is generally high in iron and is used therapeutically to treat individuals with anaemia.

Cherry blossom honey

Some people say they can definitely taste cherries in this mild, tangy honey, but that may be down to the power of suggestion. Cherry blossom honey is not very common, but you will find it wherever there are extensive cherry orchards. The colour is a lovely, rich gold – almost tangerine in some cases.

Chestnut honey

An intense, sharp aroma characterizes this medium or dark amber honey. The taste is equally forceful, essentially nutty, with a slightly bitter, almost tannic aftertaste. France and Italy are major producers. Despite the robust flavour, chestnut honey is recommended for stirring into coffee.

Clover honey

This popular, white or straw-coloured honey has a mild, sweet, butterscotch flavour. Clover honey granulates quickly, so is generally creamed or whipped. It is good for spreading on crumpets

or toast and is delicious in a banana smoothie. New Zealand, Canada and the United States are major producers.

Cotton honey

Produced in the southern states of the United States and also in large swathes of central Asia, cotton honey ranges from white to pale amber. It has a light, flowery flavour and low acidity.

Dandelion honey

Although dandelions are common plants, the honey sourced from their bright yellow flowers is quite rare. Early in the flowering season the honey is a vibrant gold colour; later batches are amber. The aroma of dandelion honey is a little ammoniacal, but if you can overcome that, the flavour is good.

Eucalyptus honey

Australia is the main producer of this clear, orange-gold honey, but it is also widely grown in southern Spain. Where honey is marketed as Australian honey, eucalyptus will be the dominant source. There are more than 500 varieties of the eucalyptus tree, all of them popular with bees. The honey has a fruity flavour, redolent of raisins, with a toffee aftertaste. It has been used in natural remedies for centuries and is believed to be good for treating chest complaints.

Fireweed honey

As its name suggests, fireweed is the first plant to appear after an area has been burned. It grows in western Canada and in the United States, as far north as Alaska. Fireweed honey is highly prized. It has a light, delicate aroma, satiny texture and light, buttery flavour.

Gallberry Honey

The tiny white blossoms of the wild gallberry, a member of the holly family, bloom for quite a short season, so the honey is much sought after by fans of its flowery flavour. The colour is pale amber with a yellowish tinge. Gallberry honey remains liquid, even at low temperatures, and is noted for its aromatic aftertaste.

Goldenrod honey

There are several varieties of goldenrod, so this American honey varies from state to state. It is unusual in that it is produced in the autumn, when there are not too many flowering plants around. Unripe goldenrod honey has an unpleasant smell that has been likened to that of rotting meat. This dissipates once the bees have finished their work but the ripened honey has a distinctive, spicy flavour that is not to everyone's taste. Goldenrod honey is widely used by commercial bakers.

Scottish beekeeper's honey

New Zealand manuka honey

FLAVOURED HONEYS

Hawthorn honey

Produced mainly in the United Kingdom, France and the United States, this honey can be anything from pale yellow to warm amber in colour. It has a fruity aroma and rich, nutty flavour.

Heather honey

Possibly the best-known variety of honey in the world, heather honey has a jelly-like consistency, even in the comb, which makes extraction difficult. The method used by most beekeepers is pressing, which is both time-consuming and messy, but heather honey has such a marvellous flavour that the effort is generally agreed to be well worthwhile. The best heather honey comes from Scotland. Depending on the source, it ranges in colour from golden, almost orange, through to a rich port-wine

shade (bell heather honey). It has a delicious flowery taste, sometimes with a light smokiness. As with a good red wine, the flavour of heather honey is said to improve with keeping.

Kamahi honey

The tree that is the source of this honey is sacred to the Maori people of New Zealand. Kamahi honey crystallizes rapidly, so is usually sold in its creamed state. It has a rich, golden colour and a complex, somewhat smoky flavour with a buttery aftertaste.

Kiawe honey

This rare white organic honey comes from Hawaii. The unheated, unfiltered honey is so sought-after that each year's crop is sold almost before the bees have harvested the nectar.

In addition to pure honeys, there is a market for honey with an extra ingredient, such as ginger, whisky, or nuts. Fresh apricots or strawberries are also packed in honey. Honey is hygroscopic so it will absorb moisture from its surroundings. The fruit immersed in the honey dries out to some extent, intensifying its flavour and giving it a slightly chewy quality. Spices such as nutmeg, cloves, anise or allspice are also used to flavour honey.

To make your own flavoured honey at home, choose a base honey with a mild, unobtrusive flavour. Pure natural blossom honey would be ideal. To flavour the contents of one 450g/1lb jar, pour the honey into a heavy pan, stir in the chosen ingredient and heat gently for 10 minutes. Do not let the honey approach boiling point. Remove from the heat, cover and leave to stand for 2 hours. Strain the honey into the clean jar, cover and label.

VANILLA Cut a vanilla pod or bean in half lengthways and scrape out the seeds. Add these to the honey. When pouring the strained honey back into the jar, halve and add the pieces of empty pod.

SPICE Add 15ml/1 tbsp allspice berries.

CITRUS Add 15ml/1 tbsp grated orange or lemon rind.

GINGER Add a 5cm/2in knob fresh ginger, peeled and thinly sliced. Add chopped or sliced candied ginger to the jar, if you like.

Spanish orange honey

Tasmanian leatherwood honey

Like rapeseed honey, kiawe honey crystallizes rapidly. It must be removed from the comb at precisely the right moment. If taken too soon the water content will be too high and it may ferment; if left for too long, it will set solid. Thick and spreadable, kiawe honey has a delicate tropical flavour.

Lavender honey

Bees love lavender. Walk past a field in full flower and your ears will register the hum of thousands of happy bees, harvesting the nectar for what will become a delectable honey. Lavender honey is golden in colour, with a delicate aromatic flavour. It is sweet but relatively subtle, making it a good choice for cooking as it will not dominate.

Lehua honey

Connoisseurs of honey rave about the clean, fruity flavour of this rare Hawaiian speciality. Its source is nectar from the beautiful red flowers of the ohia tree. It is said to have a slightly salty aftertaste.

Lime/Linden/Basswood honey

All these types of honey come from trees that are members of the same family, Tilia. The common British variety, often seen in public gardens, is *Tilia europaea*. In Europe the same tree is called the linden, while an American

Heather honey

species is known as the basswood. Whatever the tree is called, the honey is superb. The colour – water white to pale yellow, with a greenish tinge – is not particularly exciting, but the aroma is lovely. The flavour has been likened to that of green apples with a touch of mint, and it has a definite aftertaste. Lime honey is slow to granulate.

Longan honey

Also known as dragon's eye fruit, the longan is widely cultivated in southern China, Thailand and Vietnam. Longan honey is medium to dark amber in colour, with a sweet, fruity flavour redolent of peaches.

Mesquite honey

Pale and delicately flavoured, mesquite is the most important monofloral honey produced in Mexico. The flavour has been described as citrus with a suggestion of woodsmoke. The latter is not surprising, since mesquite wood chips are widely used for barbecues.

Onion honey

One of the few honeys whose aroma is so strong that the source is undeniable. Fortunately the onion smell disappears after a few weeks, although the flavour of onion can still be detected when the pale golden honey is tasted.

Orange blossom honey

With its unmistakable citrus perfume and flavour, this is a delicious and very popular honey. The colour ranges from white to pale amber. It works well in marinades, meat glazes and as a drizzle for roasted vegetables, and is a favourite topping for ice cream, porridge, and crepes.

Rapeseed/Canola honey

The startlingly bright yellow flowers of rape (also called canola) are becoming

MANUKA HONEY

There has been a lot of media attention about this honey, most of it deserved. It is famous not for its flavour (although it does taste delicious) but for its proven antibacterial qualities. Manuka honey is produced exclusively in New Zealand, from nectar gathered from the flowers of the manuka bush (*Leptospermum scoparium* above), which grows in unpolluted areas of both North and South Island.

All honey contains hydrogen peroxide, which is a weak acid with antibacterial and anti-fungal properties. Manuka honey is no exception; it also contains a mystery phytochemical that increases its efficacy still further. For want of a better description, it has been called UMF, which simply stands for Unique Manuka Factor. When compared with a standard antiseptic, phenol (carbolic acid), active manuka honey performs extremely well. It has been claimed that it even tackles antibiotic-resistant strains of bacteria, such as MRSA.

However, it is important to note that manuka honey may only be labelled 'active' after rigorous testing. Active manuka honey sold as a foodstuff and labelled 10+ will have the same antibacterial properties as a 10 per cent phenol solution. Medical manuka honey, which should only be used externally, can be up to 20+ although 18+ is a more generally recommended strength.

Citrus-infused honey

Mint-infused honey

Ginger honey

a familiar sight in many parts of the world. The set honey is white to amber and tends to be very sweet because of the high level of glucose, which makes it granulate very quickly. Rapeseed honey is used for blending and in baked goods.

Rubber honey

Rubber plantations in Sri Lanka hum with the sound of bees during the nectar flow. This occurs precisely three weeks after all leaves have dropped from the trees, making it relatively easy for beekeepers to predict when to introduce their hives. The golden or amber honey is very sweet.

Leatherwood honey

The strong, spicy, floral flavour of this unusual honey is not to everyone's taste, but it is very popular with cooks, as it is a great partner for savoury foods like chicken and lamb. The colour is a vibrant, golden yellow and the texture is creamy. Pure leatherwood honey has an enduring aftertaste that gourmets love, but those who prefer a milder flavour can opt for a blended version.

Rosemary honey

This is a very pale honey with a subtle, herby aroma. It comes from the mountains of Catalonia in eastern Spain and the lavender fields of Provence.

Sunflower honey

A warm, yellow colour, sunflower honey sets soon after being removed from the comb. The set honey is thick and creamy. It is widely produced and is especially popular in France and Italy. The flavour is not too sweet, with a light lemon tang.

Thyme honey

The most famous thyme honey is Hymettus, named after a mountain in ancient Greece whose thyme bushes produced honey of such quality that it was called the food of the gods. Thyme honey has a robust herbal flavour. It is golden in colour, with a reddish tinge.

Tupelo honey

The tupelo or pepperidge tree is native to eastern North America and also grows in southern Asia. In northern Florida hives are kept on platforms along the river swamps. Tupelo honey is golden in colour, with a greenish cast. It is much sought-after because of its lovely floral perfume and complex, somewhat fruity flavour and aftertaste. The honey has such a high ratio of fructose to glucose that it is very slow to crystallize.

Rosemary honey

Thyme honey

Vanilla honey

HONEY FOR HEALTH AND HEALING

There is nothing new about the link between honey and health. People the world over have long recognized honey's therapeutic qualities. Honey is just a concentrated solution of sugars in water, but it also contains amino acids, proteins, minerals and vitamins. Nutritionally, these are insignificant, but they appear to play a part in helping some medical conditions. There is increasing evidence of honey's efficacy in treating wounds and burns, and manuka honey is an effective antibacterial agent.

Left: Honey and lemon is a tried and tested remedy for sore throats owing to the antiseptic and antibacterial properties of honey.

AN ANCIENT AND MODERN REMEDY

Ancient Sumerians, Greeks, Egyptians and Phoenicians all used honey for healing. It played, and still plays, an important role in both Ayurvedic and traditional Islamic medicine.

None of the current research into the benefits of honey would unduly surprise the ancient Egyptians, for whom honey was an everyday remedy. Transcripts of some of the earliest records, papyruses dating back four thousand years or more, list honey as a prime ingredient in prescriptions for hundreds of conditions. For stomach pain, constipation and urinary retention, patients were advised to take honey orally, while pastes and ointments were made up for the treatment of ulcers, sores and wounds. Practitioners in both Sumeria and Egypt routinely used salves made from honey to promote healing after ear-piercing and circumcision.

Honey was also used to treat burns. One practice, used by the ancient Egyptians and being revived today, was to impregnate strips of linen with honey and place them over the affected area. The honey promoted healing and prevented sepsis from setting in.

Honey is an anti-inflammatory, and Egyptians used it for the treatment of strains and stiff joints. Their physicians prescribed a honey salve for eye infections and also recommended honey for the treatment of ulcers. Honey was even prescribed as a cure for baldness, although its efficacy in this area has not been proven.

Honey and the ancients

The ancient Greeks liked to eat honey, but they used it medicinally as well. Hippocrates prescribed honey for ulcers and sores. Aristotle claimed that those who regularly ate honey lived longer, a belief with which the philosopher Democritus, concurred. We are told that he lived for over a hundred years and attributed his great age in an era where many died young to a daily massage with olive oil and a regular diet of honey. Al-Razi, the famous Persian philosopher and physician, commended honey and vinegar for the treatment of various disorders, including gum disease and skin irritation. His belief in the efficacy of honey was not unusual in the Muslim world. The Qur'an, or Koran, the Islamic holy book, devotes an entire chapter to bees and honey, describing the latter as "a drink diverse of hues, where is healing for mankind."

Chinese medicine

Honey is also highlighted in Chinese traditional medicine. Li Shizhen, who recorded the formulations of over a thousand herbal medicines during the Ming Dynasty, suggested that medicinal herbs should be roasted with honey to improve their effectiveness. For a wheezy cough, the bulbs of a certain type of lily were ground to a powder with coltsfoot flowers, then bound with honey.

The advent of antibiotics

Honey continued to be used regularly until the early 20th century, when more sophisticated medical treatments and the discovery of antibiotics caused it to fall from favour. In 1910 it was still being recommended for a variety of minor medical conditions.

The discovery of penicillin and the sulfonamide drugs diverted attention from honey for decades, but antibiotic-resistant drugs like MRSA and Group A streptococcus has put it back in the limelight. It has been claimed that manuka honey is a safe long-term treatment option until the infection is cleared.

Above: This papyrus, c.1539–1292BCE, is 18th-dynasty New Kingdom Egyptian. It describes a medicinal recipe containing honey as "another perfect remedy."

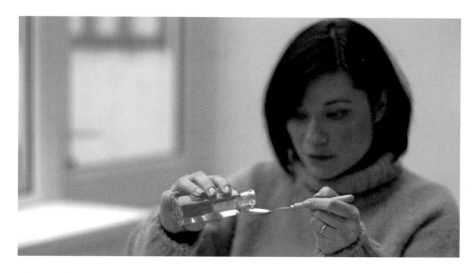

Above: When mixed with lemon juice or vinegar, honey is a tried-and-tested remedy for irritating conditions such as coughs, colds and sore throats.

How honey heals

Honey promotes healing in a variety of ways. The high sugar and low moisture levels create an osmotic effect, drawing liquid out of anything that comes into contact with it. If this is a bacterium, it is desiccated and dies. The same hygroscopic effect (ability to absorb and hold moisture) means that excess fluids are drawn from the wound site, which helps to reduce oedema (build up of fluid in tissues) and inflammation. Added to this, honey is acidic, which creates an inhospitable environment for bacteria. Finally, honey is a source of hydrogen peroxide, which is a well-known antiseptic. Dilute the honey (by moisture from a wound, for instance) and the enzyme kicks in again, giving the antibacterial activity in the honey a massive boost. The honey carries on working efficiently, even though the hydrogen peroxide is much less concentrated than a standard 3 per cent antiseptic solution. The honey is gentler and will not harm tissues.

Honey in healing

Ulcers, bedsores, abscesses, boils, burns and post-operative infections have all been treated successfully with honey and it has been used for wounds that refuse to heal, even after a year. Doctors working at Bonn University Children's Hospital reported good results after using medical honey to treat chronic wounds in children with cancer. A double-blind controlled trial among gold miners in South Africa concluded that honey was safe and as effective as a commercial healing gel in treating wounds and abrasions.

Active manuka honey is especially successful in fighting bacteria, owing to an ingredient called UMF (unique manuka factor). Manuka honey for medical purposes is packaged in tubes in New Zealand, where the manuka bush grows. It is used in burn and wound dressings, which are effective and popular with patients, since they do not stick to the wound and also have a deodorizing quality. Manuka dressings have been in use in British and Australian hospitals for some time, and have now become accepted in Canada and the United States.

Honey and hay fever

Symptoms of hay fever vary: some people have streaming eyes, runny noses and tight chests. In recent years there has been a lot of discussion about whether honey can help hay fever sufferers. The theory is if a locally produced unfiltered honey with small amounts of pollen is eaten regularly, immunity will build up to pollen from plants that grow in that area. Honeycomb is said to be even more effective than liquid honey. Anecdotal evidence also suggests that taking a teaspoon of local honey every day before the start of the hay fever season can be successful. Nettle tea, sweetened with honey, is also recommended for hay fever sufferers.

THERAPEUTIC BEE STINGS

The idea of being deliberately stung by bees may seem strange, but there are claims that bee venom can help to alleviate the symptoms of arthritis and multiple sclerosis. The theory is that the localised inflammation caused by the stings triggers an anti-inflammatory response and the release of a natural painkiller, cortisol. Patients have regular sessions, some being stung up to forty times on each occasion. There is anecdotal evidence that some sufferers have improved after they were given bee venom, however, scientific proof is scanty and MS organizations counsel individuals to check with their doctor or neurologist before considering this type of treatment. One concern is the risk of anaphylactic shock, a life-threatening allergic reaction.

HONEY REMEDIES FOR RESPIRATORY CONDITIONS

Honey is acknowledged by modern science to have antibacterial properties and deters the growth of some bacteria. It is also soothing for sore throats and coughs.

Coughs and colds

Honey is universally used for relief from bronchial ailments such as coughs and colds and has been used by Greeks, Italians and Hungarians for centuries. Together with the antibacterial properties of vinegar, it provides a powerful antidote. Take one teaspoon as needed to help quieten a cough.

INGREDIENTS

5ml/1 tsp lemon juice

5ml/1 tsp honey

5ml/1 tsp vinegar

1 Mix lemon, honey and vinegar.

2 Take one teaspoon every 2–3 hours or when needed.

MAKING REMEDIES

• When preparing remedies, use glass or stainless steel bowls and utensils – not wood or plastic.

• If possible use dried herbs.

• Refrigerate the mixture if no preservatives are used.

Sore throats

A mugful of this healing winter remedy, taken twice a day, will relieve and prevent sore throats, or sip a teaspoon slowly at night before going to bed.

INGREDIENTS

1.5ml/¼ tsp cayenne pepper

2.5ml/½ tsp ground ginger

15ml/1 tbsp honey

1 Mix together all the ingredients in a cup or mug.

2 Fill up with hot water.

3 Take one sip at a time.

LARYNGITIS

To make a drink to soothe a sore throat: Peel a 2.5-cm/1-in piece of fresh root ginger. Slice it very thinly and discard the woody centre of the ginger. Place 6–8 ginger shavings in a cup and add boiling water to fill the cup. Stir in 15ml/1 tbsp honey. Leave to stand until lukewarm before drinking, or if you prefer, chill and then drink cold.

Respiratory problems

Honey is believed to help relieve hay fever, and it may help the immune system achieve a better resistance to airborne allergies.

INGREDIENTS

5ml/1 tsp honey

2.5ml/½ tsp ground ginger

2.5ml/½ tsp crushed garlic

1 In a small bowl, mix together the honey, ginger and garlic.

2 Take with a teaspoon or dilute in a cup of water.

HAY FEVER

Pollen has been effectively used throughout the ages to relieve asthma sufferers. The treatment consisted of giving small amounts of the allergen that stimulated the asthmatic's immune system to produce antibodies, to fight the allergic reaction. Pollen is also useful for reducing the effects of hay fever; it must be taken six weeks or more before and during the length of the season.

HONEY REMEDIES FOR INTERRUPTED SLEEP

Whether sleep is disrupted by insomnia or by bedwetting, regular use of a spoonful of honey at bedtime may help remedy the condition.

Bedwetting

A tablespoon of honey given at bedtime is an old remedy used to reduce and put a stop to bedwetting. No liquids for three hours before going to bed will also help.

INGREDIENTS

15ml/1 tbsp honey

1 Swallow the honey.

2 Brush teeth before going to bed.

Insomnia

The route to a good night's sleep is to drink a tranquillizing beverage just before bedtime.

Mild or transient insomnia can be helped with natural remedies, however if the sleeplessness is chronic it could be caused by an underlying problem that needs medical attention, such as depression or heart disease.

Camomile has a component called chrysin that can promote sleep and can be used in conjunction with honey to relieve insomnia.

INGREDIENTS

5ml/1 tsp honey
a handful of fresh or dried mint leaves
250ml/8fl oz/1 cup camomile tea

1 Add the honey and the mint leaves to the camomile tea.

2 Leave to soak for a while to extract the mint flavour.

3 Strain the tea into a jug and discard the leaves. Sip a cup of the tea just before going to bed each evening.

SEDATIVE

Honey has a mild sedative effect and it holds fluid in a child's body while he or she sleeps. Honey should never be given to infants under the age of one because it contains bacteria that can be dangerous to infants (but harmless to adults and older children).

HONEY REMEDIES FOR EXPECTANT MOTHERS

Two common complaints during pregnancy are anaemia and morning sickness. For relief try the simple remedies here, but if severe, always consult your doctor for advice.

Anaemia

Women who are vegetarian are often affected by anaemia because they are unable to increase their iron intake by eating meat products. However, they can introduce more iron into their diet by eating nettles. Pick only young nettles that grow away from roads. Always wear rubber gloves to handle the nettles.

INGREDIENTS

10ml/2 tsp honey
200g/8oz/4 cups young nettle tops

1 Steam the nettle tops for a few minutes until they are limp.

2 Drain the nettle tops and transfer them to a serving plate, then drizzle with the honey.

Morning sickness

This common condition affects 60 to 80 per cent of all women during their first trimester. A new research study has shown that a mixture of ginger and honey is a safe and effective way to treat morning sickness. If the sickness is severe, omit the bran and add the honey and ginger to spring water and take as a drink.

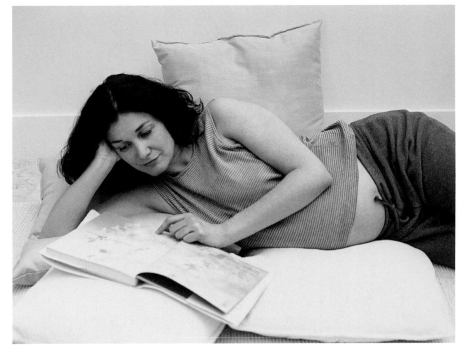

INGREDIENTS

15ml/1 tbsp honey
5ml/1 tsp root ginger, peeled
  and sliced
bran (or water if the sickness is severe)

1 Mix the honey and ginger in a bowl.

2 Add the bran and eat as a cereal.

HEARTBURN

Many pregnant women suffer from heartburn. For relief, mix 5ml/1 tsp honey with a glass of milk to neutralize excess acid.

HONEY REMEDIES FOR DIGESTIVE PROBLEMS

Honey is easily digested and has long been recognized as a remedy for stomach or intestinal problems. If someone is feeling off-colour, it gives a quick lift and improves the appetite.

Diarrhoea

This remedy for diarrhoea or vomiting, or both, works fast. If you only feel able to take liquids, just drink a glass of barley water with a teaspoon of honey added. As the ingredients are easily available, it provides quick relief for stomach upsets.

INGREDIENTS

225g/8oz/1 cup natural (plain) yogurt

15ml/1 tbsp honey

1 Stir the yogurt and honey together.

2 Eat the remedy when required.

HANGOVERS

Dr Martensen-Larsen, a leading expert on alcoholism, believes that honey aids the recovery from hangovers by blocking the route of alcohol to the brain, raising blood sugar levels and stimulating the elimination of waste and toxins. Mix 250ml/8fl oz/1 cup dandelion or nettle tea with 10ml/2 tsp honey. Stir and drink.

Stomach problems

Often the cause of stomach upsets is the *heliocobacter pylori* bacteria. Honey is known to inhibit the growth of this strain, so much so that it is sometimes advised for the relief of ulcers. It is administered each evening before bedtime. Nettle, used in this remedy because it is a natural diuretic, also stimulates the digestive system to combat any problems.

INGREDIENTS

250ml/8fl oz/1 cup nettle tea

10ml/2 tsp honey

1 Make a cup of nettle tea in a heatproof glass or mug.

2 Stir in the honey to sweeten.

STOMACH ACHE

Mix 15ml/1 tbsp honey with 15ml/1 tbsp lemon or 10ml/ 2 tsp cider vinegar. Add hot water and stir well before drinking. This drink can relieve stomach ache and indigestion.

Travel sickness

Ginger has an anti-emetic property owing to its aromatic oil, which also gives ginger its flavour. A flask of ginger tea infused with honey, or water flavoured with ginger, is useful for passengers prone to travel sickness.

INGREDIENTS

15ml/1 tbsp honey

15ml/1 tbsp ground ginger or 2.5cm/1in fresh root ginger, peeled and sliced

1 litre/1¾ pints/4 cups ginger tea or hot water

1 Mix the honey and ginger together.

2 Add to ginger tea or hot water and decant to a flask. If using fresh ginger, remove and discard.

HONEY REMEDIES FOR STRESSFUL CONDITIONS

Honey is believed to be a stabilizer, calming highs and helping through low points. Because it is made of simple sugars, honey is easily digested and quickly increases energy levels.

Nerves

A tablespoon of ginseng elixir every day before breakfast or a cup of ginseng and honey in water will relax the nerves and help in the recovery of any damage to the nervous system, in preparation for the pressures of the day ahead.

INGREDIENTS

5ml/1 tsp powdered ginseng

5ml/1 tsp honey

250ml/8fl oz/1 cup hot water

1 Mix the ginseng and honey together, then add the hot water.

2 Allow to stand for 1 minute before drinking.

LISTLESSNESS

Reach for the honey instead of a chocolate bar if you are running out of steam. The fructose and glucose in honey are easily digested and will give a rapid boost. Try a spoonful of honey before a gym workout. After an energetic session, refuel with a banana and honey sandwich.

Hot flushes

These can be an embarrassing symptom of the menopause, lasting months and sometimes years. The face flushes in colour followed by drenching sweat and an aftermath of cold and clamminess. It can be relieved by wearing light clothes and keeping a flow of air through the house or office. Regular drinks of this mix can relieve symptoms, and the sage content can help with excess sweating and the rebalancing of hormones.

INGREDIENTS

15ml/1 tbsp honey

10ml/2 tsp lemon juice

10ml/2 tsp dried sage

5ml/1 tsp dried angelica

1 litre/1¾ pints/4 cups water

1 Put the honey, lemon juice, sage and angelica in a pan with the water. Bring to the boil and simmer over a low heat for 5–10 minutes. Leave to cool.

2 Strain and pour the mixture into a bottle. Refrigerate until required then drink regularly to relieve the symptoms.

Low energy

This tonic will lift the spirits and energy levels according to traditional Chinese medicine. The following infusion, to be taken as needed, will stimulate the circulatory system, increase the efficiency of the body's blood and lymph flow and increase the feeling of wellbeing.

INGREDIENTS

1 litre/1¾ pints/4 cups cider vinegar or
  herbal tea of choice

15ml/1 tbsp finely chopped onion

2 cloves garlic, finely chopped

15ml/1 tbsp fresh ginger, peeled and sliced

1 jalepeño pepper, seeded and chopped

5ml/1 tsp grated horseradish

15ml/1 tbsp honey

1 Mix the cider vinegar, the chopped onion, garlic, ginger, jalepeño pepper, horseradish and honey in a saucepan.

2 Bring to the boil and simmer for about 10 minutes.

3 Cool, strain and store in the refrigerator.

Migraine and headaches

Caused by a tightening of the soft tissue covering the skull, migraines and headaches are often triggered by stress and hormonal changes, which can be aggravated by foods such as chocolate and red wine. An infusion of calming herbs and tea, together with nutritious honey to sweeten it, can help calm this tension. To prevent an attack of migraine, take 10ml/2 tsp honey at mealtimes.

Tension

The potassium in honey is thought to be a relaxant, and celery contains active compounds called pthalides, which aid the relaxation of the muscles of the arteries that regulate blood pressure. At the same time the amount of stress hormones are lowered so that tension is reduced. A tablespoon of this relaxant at mealtimes can have a very beneficial effect in promoting relaxation and reducing nervous tension.

INGREDIENTS

4 celery sticks

15ml/1 tbsp honey

15ml/1 tbsp water

1 Chop the celery into small pieces, then liquidize with the honey and water until well blended. Add a little more water, if necessary, to make a smooth drink.

2 Pour some relaxant into a glass and refrigerate the remainder until required.

INGREDIENTS

10ml/2 tsp dried melissa

10ml/2 tsp dried peppermint

10ml/2 tsp dried yarrow

5ml/1 tsp dried camomile

10ml/2 tsp honey

475ml/16floz/2 cups green tea

1 Mix the dried melissa, peppermint, yarrow, camomile and honey into the green tea. Leave to soak for 5–10 minutes.

2 Strain, transfer the remedy to a glass and take a small cup every 2 hours.

HONEY REMEDIES FOR SKIN CONDITIONS

Honey is known for is anti-microbial activity and in some cases it appears to work quicker than conventional treatments, particularly for burns and bedsores.

Bedsores

Rhubarb has been used medicinally since 3000BCE, and with honey it helps to heal bedsores when a paste is applied to the affected area. Cook a stick of rhubarb until soft and strain the juice.

INGREDIENTS

15ml/1 tbsp honey

15ml/1 tbsp rhubarb juice

clean lint

1 In a small bowl, mix the honey and rhubarb juice together.

2 Spread the paste on a piece of clean lint and apply to the sore.

Burns

Research shows that burns treated with honey-soaked gauze heal twice as quickly as those employing orthodox methods, and scarring was reduced. Honey inhibits fungi and bacteria.

INGREDIENTS

15ml/1 tbsp honey or propolis

sterilized gauze

tape

1 Spread honey or propolis on a piece of sterilized gauze.

2 Apply the gauze to the burn, then secure with tape.

Grazes and sores

This simple remedy uses a dab of honey, which is sealed with petroleum or royal jelly. The honey kills the bacteria and speeds healing of the graze or sore, while the jelly excludes air and helps to keep the skin sterile.

INGREDIENTS

5ml/1 tsp honey

a little petroleum jelly or royal jelly

1 Cover the graze or sore with a small dab of honey.

2 Seal with petroleum or royal jelly and leave overnight.

Sunburn

As well as being good at treating burns, honey also helps to heal sunburn. Used straight from the refrigerator, this cream makes a very soothing after-sun treatment, applied to affected areas. Any redness will be calmed by the anti-inflammatory properties of the aloe vera, which also acts as an analgesic.

INGREDIENTS

20ml/4 tsp beeswax granules
60ml/4 tbsp honey
10ml/2 tsp aloe vera or wheat germ oil

1 Put the beeswax granules with the honey and aloe vera gel or oil in a warmed bowl.

2 Stir well to mix and, if necessary, warm again in a bain marie to melt the beeswax. Transfer the mixture to a wide-necked jar and gently smooth on to skin to soothe sunburn.

Cuts

Because honey is rich in sugar, vitamins, minerals and enzymes including inhibine, which helps to prevent infection, it can be used as an antibiotic ointment for wounds. A research trial published in the British Journal of Plastic Surgery proved that as germs did not survive in honey, it proved to be a faster wound healer than a specifically trialled hospital product.

INGREDIENTS

5ml/1 tsp honey or propolis
cotton wool balls, lint and bandage

1 Soak cotton wool balls in water, then use them to clean the wound. Hold them in tongs to keep sterile.

2 Use a cotton bud to apply honey or propolis to the wound. Cover the area with a sterile wrap or sterilized lint followed by a bandage. Check the next day and replace if necessary.

Dry skin

As well as having antibacterial and antibiotic properties, honey has a healing and moisturizing effect on dry skin, stimulating regrowth and renewal. This simple exfoliating remedy can be made using ingredients from the kitchen storecupboard.

INGREDIENTS

30ml/2 tbsp honey
30ml/2 tbsp olive oil
30ml/2 tbsp natural (plain) yogurt
45ml/3 tbsp pinhead oatmeal

1 Mix all the ingredients together to make a paste and apply gently to the face, avoiding the eye area.

2 Leave the paste on for 5 minutes, then wash off with warm water. Finish by splashing the face with cool water to refresh the skin and boost the circulation to the face.

HONEY REMEDIES FOR WEIGHT LOSS AND ENERGY

Taking honey is reputed to induce a feeling of fullness so is a good food to help slimming. Honey also gives a boost to energy and is thought to support the immune system.

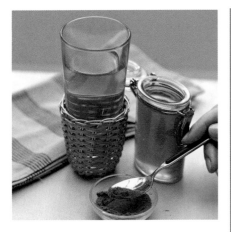

Slimming

Honey mixed with cinnamon is claimed to help in weight loss. Unlike sugar, honey contains vitamins and minerals, which are believed to help in fat and cholesterol metabolism. Using honey instead of sugar can reduce calories.

INGREDIENTS

15ml/1 tbsp honey

2.5ml/½ tsp ground cinnamon

1 Mix the ingredients in a cup.

2 Add boiling water and stir. Cool a little before drinking.

Energy boost and immune support

Fruit sugars in honey are easily digested to provide a natural energy boost for the body. Honey-based drinks are an alternative to those that enhance athletic performance, at the same time replacing body minerals lost through perspiration.

INGREDIENTS

45ml/3 tbsp honey

5ml/1 tsp each salt and cider vinegar

1 Mix the ingredients together.

2 Add to a flask with water. Shake well.

HONEY REMEDIES FOR AILMENTS IN OLDER LIFE

As people age, ailments and health problems tend to appear. Remedies using honey and beeswax that have been tried and tested over decades can offer relief in a natural way.

Arthritis

There have been many documented cases of arthritis sufferers finding relief from wax treatments to affected parts. The hot wax eases stiffness caused by inflammation of the joints.

INGREDIENTS

2.25kg/5lb beeswax

475ml/16fl oz/2 cups mineral oil

1 Heat the oven to 100°C/200°/Gas ¼. Place the beeswax and mineral oil in an ovenproof dish and heat in the oven until the wax has melted. Stir occasionally to blend the wax and oil.

2 Carefully remove from the oven and allow to cool until the mixture is still warm but not uncomfortably hot. Dip the part of the body to be treated into the wax mixture then withdraw when it is coated in wax. If you are treating the hand, keep the fingers apart.

3 Repeat until there is a thick coating, then leave in the wax until the mixture cools. Remove and peel off the wax.

Hair restorer

Once a day, massaging the scalp rigorously with the fingertips in a shampooing action will activate the sebaceous glands, stimulate the hair follicles and generally improve the circulation of blood to the affected area. This preparation, used weekly, will nourish the hair with vitamins and minerals that may be lacking in the diet. You should start to see a marked improvement after a few weeks and the hair should look glowing and healthy.

INGREDIENTS

5ml/1 tsp honey

2.5ml/½ tsp olive oil

5ml/1 tsp dried sage

90ml/6 tbsp mineral water

1 Add the honey, olive oil and sage to the mineral water and mix well.

2 Massage the mixture into the scalp for a few minutes.

3 Leave the preparation on the head for about 30 minutes, then wash off.

Gall stones

Caused by a build-up of calcifications in the gall bladder, gall stones can be small and easy to pass, or may be painful and require medical attention. An old country remedy to reduce the likelihood of stones increasing in size is to drink a measure of this herbal mix daily.

INGREDIENTS

1 litre/1¾ pints/4 cups water

25ml/1½ tbsp honey

15ml/1 tbsp ground ginger

25ml/1½ tbsp lemon balm

25ml/1½ tbsp freshly chopped parsley

15g/½ oz liquorice root

1 Boil the water in a pan and add the honey, ginger, lemon balm, parsley and liquorice root.

2 Bring to the boil, then simmer until the volume is reduced by half.

3 Leave to cool, then strain into a bottle and store in the refrigerator.

4 Drink a glass of the mixture every day.

NATURAL BEAUTY WITH HONEY AND BEESWAX

Honey has been used as a beauty preparation since the days of the ancient Romans – and for a lot longer than that. In the days of the pharaohs, honey was used in face washes, hair rinses and potions. To promote soft skin and a radiant complexion, a honey mask was applied by Egyptian ladies, and beeswax was used in wrinkle creams and pomades. The qualities of honey and beeswax are still recognized and they are just as relevant today in beauty products.

Left: Beeswax is used to set this solid perfume, which can be divided into small containers and carried in a handbag.

HONEY PREPARATIONS THROUGH THE AGES

Honey and beeswax have long been used in cosmetics as part of a natural beauty regime. Even the most sensitive skins seem to find honey soothing, and beeswax has an emollient effect.

Honey has been acknowledged worldwide as a wonderfully useful ingredient in beauty preparations. Its healing properties and its ability to attract and retain moisture make it a natural ingredient for beauty products, including face creams, shampoos and hand lotions. Honey is popular in anti-aging products for skin because it replenishes lost moisture.

Honey in Rome and Egypt

Roman women experimented with honey-based creams, perfumes and potions and Cleopatra was reputed to use milk and honey in her bath to

Below: As well as having emollient properties, beeswax creates a harder soap that lasts for longer.

cleanse and moisturize her skin. An Egyptian perfume that found favour with no less a luminary than Pliny the Elder combined almond oil and olive oil with honey and rare spices. The Roman version was given the name 'metopium.' High-born Roman women spent a lot of time and effort on their appearance. Poppea, Nero's wife, was so taken with the ass's milk and honey formula that she bathed in the mixture twice a day.

Honey mixed with lentils, wheat, narcissus and eggs was used as a face mask to lighten the skin. To make the hair lighter – and improve its condition – a massage with a mixture of honey and lemon juice was recommended. To lessen the appearance of wrinkles, women used a paste of bean meal, barley meal and raw egg. According to Ovid, if this mixture was dried and ground, then mixed with melted beeswax and honey, it would make a cream that would keep the skin beautifully smooth.

Honey in the 17th century

Throughout succeeding centuries, honey was used in cosmetics, perfumes and beauty treatments. It was not merely the preserve of the rich; any woman who kept bees could utilize some of their bounty to make beauty preparations for her own use. Honey found its way into hand creams, body lotions and all manner of mixtures. In the 17th century, Queen Anne, who was described as having a 'soft and comely visage', started a fashion for honey hair rinses when it was revealed that

Above: Since ancient times, honey has been used in beauty routines.

she owed her lustrous dark curls to applications of honey and olive oil. Victorian women of standing sneered at 'painted ladies' but were happy to improve upon nature with a few simple honey preparations: a slick of honey salve for moist, glossy lips or a mask of honey, oatmeal and egg yolk to keep the complexion smooth and silky.

Why honey?

Honey has a number of attributes that make it highly suitable as an ingredient in cosmetics and beauty preparations. In addition to the antibacterial properties already mentioned, which make it a useful preparation for spotty skins, honey is a natural humectant. The antioxidants in honey help to repair damaged skin and improve general tone and elasticity. They are particularly helpful in protecting against damage by UV rays.

Honey also has keratolytic qualities, which means that it encourages the removal of dead skin cells from the surface of the skin, especially when used with alpha hydroxy acids (AHAs). AHAs are important ingredients in skin-care preparations as they promote exfoliation and give the skin a younger, more glowing appearance. Milk contains AHAs, so the milk and honey combination used by Cleopatra had a scientific basis.

Another advantage of using honey is that it does not irritate, so is suitable even for sensitive skins.

Honey is widely used today in commercial cosmetics. At one time the proportion of honey to other ingredients was deliberately kept low, to reduce stickiness, but with modern techniques and the addition of emulsifiers, the

Above: Herbal tea made with honey and lemon is a good detoxifier. It cleanses the system and helps to keep the skin clear and free from spots and blemishes.

honey element can be as high as 70 per cent, giving maximum moisturizing benefits. It is also blended with essential oils in many preparations.

The honey spa

Skin care treatments using honey have become very popular at spas and beauty clinics. Some spas offer honey-based foot treatments consisting of a pedicure and sugar and honey exfoliation, then a hot milk and honey foot soak.

You can bathe in milk and honey, in the style of Cleopatra. Milk makes the skin soft and smooth and honey nourishes and moisturizes, while honey massages take the tension out of muscles and soothe and rehydrate the skin. Other popular treatments include

Right: Beeswax and honey make a soothing and moisturizing body cream.

rose and honey body wraps. You don't have to go to a spa to indulge yourself, however. You can give yourself a top-to-toe makeover using ready-made preparations containing honey or you can make up your own mixtures at home, following the natural beauty recipes in this chapter.

SENSITIVITY TEST

Although honey has the power to calm tender or inflamed skin and is generally non-irritating, and seems to agree with the most sensitive or troubled skin, other ingredients in ready-prepared mixes may not be as suitable for you. It is a good idea to always do a sensitivity test by dabbing a little on the back of your hand or behind your ear. To avoid over-exposure, do not use one mixture exclusively.

HONEY FOR SCENTS AND BATHING

Using honey in a bath balm will leave the skin smooth and soothed, combating any dryness. Beeswax is the base for the solid perfume, which is easy to carry around without spilling.

Honey and vanilla bath oil

If you prefer bubbles in your bath you can replace 100ml/3½fl oz/½ cup of oil with liquid soap or 115g/4oz of hand-made soap. Have a different oil each day of the week by replacing the vanilla and lemon with essential oils. Try lavender for relaxation, patchouli for a heavily scented, pampering bath or a mix to suit.

INGREDIENTS

350ml/12fl oz/1½ cups jojoba or sweet
  almond oil
120ml/4fl oz/½ cup honey
15ml/1 tbsp vanilla extract
15ml/1 tbsp lemon juice

1 Pour all the oil into a suitable bowl and slowly add the other ingredients, stirring gently. You may wish to slightly warm the honey beforehand to speed up the blending process.

2 Put the mixture into a coloured bottle with a tight-fitting lid to stop deterioration from exposure to light. Remember to shake the bottle gently before using.

3 Store the oil in a cool, dark place.

Solid perfume

Add your favourite essential oil or scent to this perfume. You may wish to make a large quantity and decant into several small containers or to make small quantities with different perfumes, so the recipe is given in parts. For example a small 6g pot would consist of 3g oil, 2g wax and 1g essential oil or scent.

INGREDIENTS

3 parts jojoba or sweet almond oil
2 parts beeswax, preferably white
1 part essential oil or scent

1 In a bain marie, heat the jojoba or almond oil, beeswax and oils or scent.

2 Stir with a wooden spoon and pour into a jar or container.

SCENTED OILS

Ring the changes with different essential oils. The use of grapefruit would uplift the spirits, whereas ylang ylang and bergamot would create a very sensual smell.

Bath bombs

These are very easy to make, are fun and will leave the bathroom filled with a wonderful aroma. Simply drop them in the tub and the ingredients will explode, releasing all their scent and petals. Children suddenly find bathing a time to look forward to and can have fun making their own bombs. Wrapped in coloured cellophane, foil or brown paper and tied with ribbon or raffia, they make inexpensive, attractive gifts.

INGREDIENTS

225g/8oz/1 cup bicarbonate of soda (baking soda)
90g/3½oz/½ cup citric acid
15ml/1 tbsp honey
few drops vanilla extract or essential oil
150ml/¼ pint/⅔ cup witch hazel, decanted into a spray bottle
15ml/1 tbsp dried herbs, petals, or food colouring (optional)

1 Mix the bicarbonate of soda and citric acid in a bowl until blended.

2 Add the honey and vanilla or essential oil, to perfume the mixture.

3 Add any optional ingredients, such as the herbs or petals and a chosen food colouring. Work quickly to avoid the bomb exploding prematurely. Using the witch hazel spray, spritz the mixture until wet and stir with your hand until it reaches a dough-like consistency.

4 If the mixture starts to fizz, add a little more of the bicarbonate of soda, which will take up the extra witch hazel. Press the mixture into a mould such as an ice-cube tray, or roll into balls and place on a tray or board. Leave overnight to dry out thoroughly.

5 For a special gift, make a large bomb, wrap it in cellophane and tie a pretty ribbon around it.

TIP

The tighter you pack the mixture into the moulds, the harder and longer lasting the bomb will turn out. As with baking recipes, after you have made the bombs a few time, you will be better able to judge the approximate quantities of the dry ingredient and the witch hazel. This will allow you to get the best consistency for your bombs.

HONEY FOR HAIRCARE

With honey and a few simple ingredients, you can make natural shampoos and conditioner for most hair types that will leave your hair clean and shining.

Normal shampoo

Many hair products today base their ingredients on natural products. One of the first of these was the famous egg shampoo based on a very old recipe that is easy to follow at home. With the addition of honey, this rich shampoo leaves the hair healthy and shiny.

INGREDIENTS

1 large egg
5ml/1 tsp honey
45ml/3 tbsp soap flakes

1 Separate the yolk and white of the egg. Whisk the egg white until frothy.

2 Blend in the yolk and honey and add the soap flakes. Wet the hair with warm water – do not use hot water as this may scramble the egg.

3 Massage half the shampoo mixture into the hair and scalp and rinse well with water. Apply the remaining mixture and leave on the hair for a few minutes before rinsing out thoroughly with warm water.

Frequent-use shampoo

The addition of camomile makes this a favourite for regular shampooing.

INGREDIENTS

4 teabags of camomile tea or one handful
  camomile flowers
350ml/12fl oz/1½ cups boiling water
60ml/4 tbsp soap flakes
30ml/2 tbsp honey

1 Steep the teabags or flowers in the boiling water for 10 minutes.

2 Strain the liquid into a bowl and stir in the soap flakes and honey. Cool.

3 Wet the hair, then massage half of the mixture into the scalp and hair. Rinse.

HAIR TIPS

Always use a shampoo that suits your hair and before washing the hair, brush it well to remove any tangles and loosen dirt and skin cells. Rinse your hair with lukewarm water.

Anti-dandruff shampoo

To make an anti-dandruff shampoo, use a mixture of rosemary and honey. If you like, massage a little liquid into the scalp before bedtime in-between shampoos.

INGREDIENTS

5ml/1 tsp dried rosemary
5ml/1 tsp dried thyme
150ml/¼ pint/⅔ cup boiling water
15ml/1 tbsp honey
150ml/¼ pint/⅔ cup cider vinegar

1 Place the herbs in a bowl and pour over the boiling water.

2 Add the honey and mix until it is melted. Cover and allow to steep for 20 minutes.

3 Strain the mixture into a bottle or jar.

4 Add the cider vinegar and shake well to mix.

5 Wet the hair and massage in some of the shampoo. Rinse. Store the remaining shampoo in a cool, dry place.

Conditioner

Once you have made your chosen shampoo, you may need a conditioner to complete your haircare routine, particularly if your hair is dry, fine or coloured. The hair follicles need natural vitamins and minerals to feed off and if these are lacking from your diet the condition of your hair will suffer. In medieval times, honey was thought to cure baldness. This may be a little optimistic but honey definitely helps to promote the condition and manageabiity of the hair and scalp.

Honey and vinegar rinse

If your hair is in reasonably good condition but just lacks shine, give it a lift with this honey and vinegar rinse.

INGREDIENTS

5ml/1 tsp honey

1 litre/1¾ pints/4 cups hot water

5ml/1 tsp cider vinegar or lemon juice

1 Mix the ingredients together. Cool.

2 Pour over the hair as a final rinse.

INGREDIENTS

5ml/1 tsp honey

1 egg

10ml/2 tsp coconut or olive oil

1 In a plastic bowl or jug, mix together all the ingredients until blended.

2 Massage over the whole of the scalp. Wrap the head in a warm towel and leave for 30 minutes.

3 Rinse off, then shampoo as normal using a mild shampoo.

HAIR RINSES

After a honey shampoo, you can enhance your natural hair colour. Sunshine can have a fading effect on the hair, and you may wish to use natural additives in the final rinse of your haircare routine.

For medium brown to dark hair, add cider vinegar to the rinse; for fair to medium fair hair, use lemon juice. Add 25ml/1½ tbsp of cider vinegar or lemon or lime juice to 200ml/7fl oz/scant 1 cup water. Use the mixture as the final rinse.

HONEY FOR NATURAL SKIN TREATMENTS

Honey is the perfect ingredient to add to skin creams because it keeps the skin hydrated and fresh and stops it drying out. Because it is an antimicrobial agent, it also keeps the skin healthy.

Cleanser

Rosemary and beeswax cream is excellent for removing makeup and mascara and is suitable for most skin types. Make in small quantities and keep for up to one month in the refrigerator.

INGREDIENTS

12g/⅓oz beeswax

15g/½oz emulsifying wax

15ml/1 tbsp coconut oil

100ml/3½fl oz/scant ½ cup olive oil

1.5ml/¼ tsp borax

30ml/2 tbsp warm water

7.5ml/½ tbsp rosewater

5 drops rosemary essential oil

1 Melt the beeswax, emulsifying wax, coconut oil and olive oil in a bain marie or microwave.

2 In a separate bowl, dissolve the borax in the warm water.

3 Slowly add the melted oils from the first bowl, stirring constantly. When lukewarm, add the oil and rosewater. When cool, refrigerate.

Facial scrub

Using a scrub is a great way of exfoliating dead skin cells on the face and attacking oily areas where blackheads and blemishes occur. There are many varieties of ingredients that you can use to achieve this and you can have fun trying out your own versions of this base recipe. The honey and banana are rich rehydrators to counteract the abrasiveness of the scrub and will also give a scrumptious fragrance to the mix.

INGREDIENTS

120ml/4fl oz/½ cup oatmeal, coffee grains or sugar granules

30ml/2 tbsp honey

1 ripe banana

1 Mix all the ingredients together to form a thick paste.

2 Massage over the face, focusing on areas that need attention and avoiding the eyes. Leave on for a few minutes before washing off with a soft cloth and warm water, followed by a splash of astringent.

Skin tonic

The old remedy of placing a slice of cucumber over each eye to reduce any puffiness and refresh tired eyes has a new twist. Pollen promotes the healing of damaged skin, so if your skin looks a bit sluggish, a cucumber tonic is an instant brightener. The vitamin C in cucumber improves circulation, clarity and texture, leaving the skin luminous.

INGREDIENTS

½ cucumber

30ml/2 tbsp pollen granules

30ml/2 tbsp natural (plain) yogurt (optional)

1 Cut the cucumber into chunks and add the pollen granules. Mash together or whizz in a liquidizer.

2 Strain before use.

3 If you want a thicker preparation, add the natural yogurt.

4 Decant the mixture to a previously sterilized container and when cold, refrigerate until ready to use.

Face moisturizer

All lotions and creams have three main components – water, oil and an emulsifying agent that encourages the water and oil to combine. This cream contains rosewater and almond oil and the emulsifier is beeswax. Honey is added because of its moisturizing qualities and its ability to hold moisture. Essential oils are added to give a light fragrance to the cream and the addition of vitamin E oil is effective in ironing out wrinkles and fading scars on the skin.

INGREDIENTS

10g/¼oz beeswax
20ml/4 tsp almond oil
75ml/5 tbsp rosewater or distilled water
10ml/2 tsp honey
few drops of frankincense, geranium or rose
    absolute essential oils (optional)
1 vitamin E capsule (optional)

1 Heat together the beeswax and oil in a bain marie or microwave until the wax is just melted.

2 Heat together the water and honey until just under boiling. Combine with the beeswax mixture and mix together for 5 minutes.

3 Set aside until lukewarm, then add any optional ingredients. Pour into a wide-necked jar and when cool, put a lid on and store in the refrigerator.

Eye cream

Honey's ability to attract and seal in moisture is put to use in this eye cream, which leaves skin soft and supple. Make a fresh formula for each application, then gently pat the mixture on to the tissue around the eyes, avoiding dragging the skin. Once dry, remove gently by washing off with warm water. For more mature skin, add frankincense essential oil, known for its anti-ageing properties. Apply with care, making sure that you keep the mixture away from the eye directly, working only on the surrounding areas.

INGREDIENTS

15ml/1 tbsp honey
1 egg white
3–5 drops frankincense essential oil
    (optional)

1 Mix the honey with the egg white.

2 Add the essential oil, if using, and mix.

Mask

Face masks are great to help soften and clean the skin, and honey on its own or blended with a little rosewater makes a very basic mask. Manuka honey is expensive but it has excellent healing properties and is ideal for treating skin conditions. Before applying the mask, wash your face in warm water to open the pores. Spread the mask on your face, avoiding the eyes, and leave for 15–30 minutes. Wash off with a soft flannel. To make a more substantial mask, add oatmeal to the mix. Using this once a week will leave you with glowing skin.

INGREDIENTS

50g/2oz/1 cup oatmeal
30ml/1 tbsp honey
5ml/1 tsp rosewater

1 Blend the oatmeal with the honey and add the rosewater.

2 Mix until a smooth paste is formed.

HONEY FOR HAND AND NAIL CARE

Honey is one of the finest skin foods so it is often used as an ingredient in hand cream or barrier cream. It helps hands exposed to harsh weather conditions and water.

Honey and beeswax cream

The hands are very noticeable because they are always on show, and they age quickly owing to exposure to the elements. Because they are being frequently immersed in water and harsh detergents, the skin dries out faster than on other areas of the body.

Other factors such as heating and air conditioning also have a drying effect. Rough skin and premature aging can be arrested by a daily application of a cream containing honey and beeswax. The honey helps to nourish the hands and slows down the aging process, while beeswax is a good emollient and makes an excellent barrier, so that water, which dries out the hands, cannot penetrate the skin.

INGREDIENTS

10ml/2 tsp beeswax granules

30ml/2 tbsp honey

10ml/2 tsp olive oil

10 drops rose essential oil

1 Warm the beeswax granules in a bain marie until melted. Put in a bottle or flask and add the honey, olive oil and rose essential oil. Shake the bottle well to mix.

HANDY TIPS

• Always rub in hand cream after a bath or washing your hands, while the skin is still warm, so that it will sink in easily.

• Keep a bottle of hand cream near to the sink to remind you to use it after washing up. Have another bottle next to your bed so you can apply cream before you go to sleep.

• To quickly exfoliate your hands, mix some sea salt and lemon juice together, rub into the hands and rinse off. This will remove dead skin cells and soften skin.

• For a 5-minute treatment, mix 5ml/1 tsp olive oil with 5ml/1 tsp honey. Rub over the hands so they are coated with a thin layer, then wear latex gloves with cotton gloves on top. Leave overnight to allow the skin to absorb the treatment.

• To stimulate circulation, rub the palm of one hand over the back of the other hand.

2 Shake the bottle until the cream is smooth, then apply to the hands. If using it at night, wear either cotton or latex gloves overnight. The next day, rub in any cream that remains.

Cuticle softener

The cuticle is the protective layer of skin at the base of the finger or toe nail that often becomes dry and ragged as it builds up. Never cut the cuticles because they are sealed barriers that prevent infection. To make it easier to push back or remove during regular nailcare, a softener is often applied. Using a natural product containing honey has the added benefit of fighting any build up of bacteria and nourishing the nail itself. Use regularly by massaging the mixture into the cuticles and leave for a few minutes. If you want to have a more intense treatment, leave the cuticle softener on overnight and sleep in a pair of cotton gloves.

INGREDIENTS

1 lemon

5ml/1 tsp honey

5ml/1 tsp almond oil

NAIL TIPS

• When filing your nails, prevent them splitting by filing them into a square or oval shape. Don't file them low into the corners because this can weaken the nails. File gently in one long stroke, from the side to the centre of the nail. The best length for nails is just over the fingertip.

• Exposure to water causes nails to become soft and to damage easily, so wear latex gloves when washing dishes to protect your nails.

• Before gardening, drag your nails over a bar of soap because when the nails are full of the soap, there is no space for dirt. The soap can be gently scraped out when you are finished.

• Don't file your nails after a bath when they are soft and pliable or they are likely to split.

• Buff the nails once a week: any more and it will weaken them.

1 Squeeze the lemon and transfer 5ml/ 1 tsp juice to a small bowl.

2 Add the honey and almond oil to the lemon juice.

3 Whisk the ingredients until thoroughly blended together.

4 Dip each finger into the mixture. Leave for a few seconds.

5 Using a cuticle tool, push down on the cuticles very gently.

6 Massage into the nails using a circular movement until absorbed.

HONEY FOR LIPS

For the nourishing and healing of dry or chapped lips, particularly in the winter months, this balm made with beeswax and essential oil has a rich emollient effect.

It is simple to make your own lip balm to moisturize and soothe lips that have been affected by the sun and the wind, the temperature or even by illness. This balm is very easy to make and contains honey and beeswax, which are excellent for moisturizers. For a simple instant balm, just combine a drop of honey with a flavouring such as vanilla or rosewater. Either will make a quick salve for sore or chapped lips.

If your lips are flaking, gently remove any dead skin with a soft toothbrush, then apply the lip balm. Another method is to coat the lips with petroleum jelly. Leave it to work for a few minutes, then gently rub your lips with a warm damp cloth. The flakes of skin will be removed.

INGREDIENTS

30ml/2 tbsp coconut or olive oil
15ml/1 tbsp beeswax
4 drops lavender, lemon or
  peppermint essential oil
vitamin E capsule or equivalent in
  vitamin E oil

1 Mix the coconut oil, beeswax and essential oil in a bowl. Place in a bain marie, or in a pan of simmering water.

2 Blend the ingredients gently together with a spoon or spatula until the wax is completely melted.

TIPS FOR USING BEESWAX

• Beeswax melts at 147°C/64°F and should not be overheated because it then loses its aroma and becomes very brittle and liable to develop cracks when cooled.

• Beeswax is very inflammable, so always melt it in a bain marie or in a microwave, but never melt it in a pan over a flame.

• It takes about 45 seconds to melt beeswax in a microwave and 3 minutes in a bain marie.

3 Break open the vitamin E capsule, add the contents to the wax mixture and mix well. Pour the mixture into a suitable container and allow to cool and set.

HONEY FOR FRESH BREATH

Sometimes cleaning your teeth is not enough and a gargle with a mouthwash with antiseptic and antibacterial properties is needed to help fight any plaque-forming bacteria.

Often a mouth rinse is necessary for good oral hygiene. This excellent mouthwash is simply made with ingredients from your storecupboard. It is easily prepared if you would like a change from your usual product or if you prefer a natural option that is free of chemicals. Honey is a well-known antibacterial agent, as well as having antiseptic properties, so it is a perfect addition to this mouthwash. It is known that its bactericide (bacteria-killing) properties increase when diluted with water. Store in a cool place and use to rinse your mouth every morning and evening, or after you brush your teeth.

INGREDIENTS

5ml/1 tsp dried peppermint or
  dried spearmint
5ml/1 tsp dried thyme
5ml/1 tsp crushed cloves
500ml/17fl oz/generous 2 cups distilled
  water or cider vinegar
5ml/1 tsp honey
10 drops peppermint essential oil

HONEY AS AN ANTIBACTERIAL AGENT

• Honey inhibits bacterial action and thus blocks oral bacteria.

• When added to a mouthwash, honey kills germs in the mouth and cleans teeth and dentures.

• As well as freshening breath, honey helps to heal mouth ulcers.

• When used regularly, honey mouthwash will help to heal any sores in the mouth.

1 Mix the peppermint, dried thyme and crushed cloves with the water or cider vinegar. Soak for 7–10 days.

2 Strain the mixture through a sieve and reserve the liquid in a bowl. Discard the dried herbs.

3 Add the honey and the peppermint oil. Pour the mouthwash into a clean bottle or jar, ready for use.

HONEY AND BEESWAX IN THE HOUSE AND GARDEN

Beeswax is an ingredient in many common household products – candles, soaps and furniture polishes. It is used to make candles because it burns cleanly with no residue and minimal smoke; in polish it provides a smooth and protective finish for wood, and it can even be used for lubricating drawer runners and racquet handles. Soap, hand cream, bath oils and bath lotions sometimes contain beeswax because it is so softening and soothing to the skin.

Left: Candles made from beeswax burn brighter, cleaner and longer than any other type of wax candles – and they smell good too.

USING BEE PRODUCTS IN THE HOME

Beeswax and honey have been used around the house since ancient times and because they are natural products without any toxic or artificial additives, they are still popular today.

Both honey and beeswax are found together in some household products, such as soaps, while beeswax is used alone in good quality candles and polishes for wood and leather.

Soap, candles and polishes

Beeswax and honey are popular ingredients in home-made soaps because of the emollient qualities of beeswax and its ability to form a barrier to protect the skin. The addition of beeswax to home-made soap makes a hard, creamy soap with an aromatic scent that does not contain any harmful synthetic ingredients, and it is mild enough for even the most sensitive skin.

Candles made from beeswax are popular in the home because they burn brighter, hotter and longer than candles made from paraffin wax. Also, they have the advantage of being smokeless, and they do not drip. Beeswax candles create a relaxing atmosphere because they release a sweet aromatic scent that is derived from the honey and pollen that remain in the honeycomb cells.

Beeswax polishes have traditionally been used in the home to either revive distressed wood or leather, or to enhance the fine patina of wooden furniture, as well as impart a wonderfully silky, protective finish. In addition, the polish is natural with no harsh chemicals to harm the environment, and has a pleasant aroma with a hint of honey.

Small wooden balls polished with honey or beeswax can be used in closets and drawers to deter moths and to add a honeyed scent to your clothes.

Above: Beeswax is formed in hexagonal-shaped cells in the hive. Older wax is removed and is used in the manufacture of products such as soap.

Honey and beeswax will add subtle fragrance to your home, and help to enhance your health and wellbeing.

Christmas tree reviver

An unusual use of honey is for reviving and freshening a Christmas tree that is required to last through the holiday season. If the tree has no roots and you want to check the freshness of the tree, simply rub your finger over the base. If your finger feels slightly sticky, there is still sap on the stump, indicating that it has been freshly cut. If not, you can make a solution that mimics the sap of a live tree by mixing 250ml/8fl oz/1 cup honey and 200g/7oz sugar with 10 litres/2.6 gallons water. Stir well, then

pour the mixture into a bucket and stand the tree in it. This treatment helps to keep the tree perky and reduces the rate of pine needles falling off throughout the Christmas festivities.

Right: Stand your Christmas tree in a honey mixture to keep it looking festive.

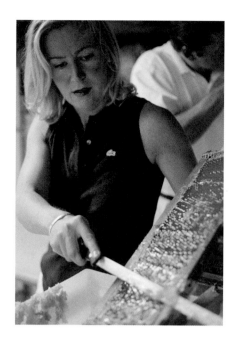

Above: A woman is trimming the wax cappings from a large hive frame to release the honey that is sealed beneath.

Above: Beeswax candles are said to be the finest because they burn brighter, hotter and cleaner than other candles.

Above: Beeswax polish gives a smooth and shiny finish to wooden furniture and has a lovely honey aroma.

GOLF CLUB GRIP WAX

Most golfers need to regrip their clubs once a year. For the occasional golfer, this can be extended by several months with regular maintenance. Waxing will prevent grips becoming slippery or cracked and improve the golfer's grip in wet conditions.

To make the grip wax, melt 50g/2oz beeswax with 5ml/1 tsp powdered resin in a bain marie. Meanwhile, create a 10cm/4in diameter tube from thick paper, or use a cardboard tube. Fill the tube with the melted mixture. Once set, use to wax the grip of golf clubs or tennis racquets, peeling the paper away as the wax is used.

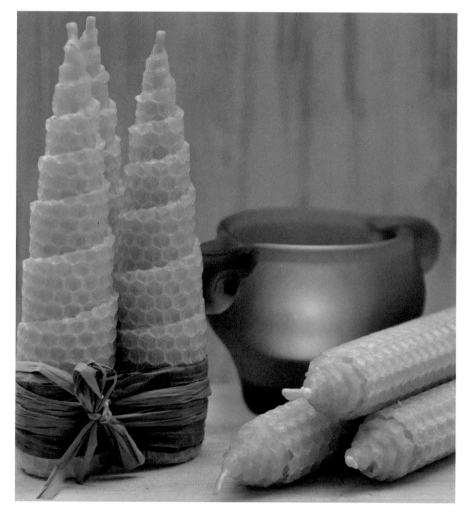

Above: Sheets of beeswax can be rolled into straight candles or spiral-shaped candles. Because they produce negative ions while burning, they leave the air fresher and cleaner.

BEESWAX POLISHES

Beeswax polish not only has a fragrant scent, it imparts a wonderful shine to leather and wooden furniture, and it is very simple to make your own regular supply at home.

Solid furniture polish

Start by making small quantities. For a soft satin shine on wood, substitute carnauba wax for the linseed oil and increase the turpentine by 100ml/3½fl oz/½ cup.

INGREDIENTS

175g/6oz/1½ cups beeswax

250ml/8fl oz/1 cup linseed oil

250ml/8fl oz/1 cup turpentine

1 Using a microwave or bain marie, warm the beeswax, linseed oil and turpentine. Mix well off the heat.

2 Pour the polish into a clean jar with a wide neck and allow to set. Apply to the item, dry and buff with a soft cloth. For best results, rub in small circles.

REMOVING BEESWAX FROM FURNITURE

If beeswax is accidentally spilled on a wooden surface, take off as much as possible, then heat the area using a hair dryer on a low setting. Once the wax liquifies, wipe clean with a dry cloth.

Liquid polish

For those who prefer a liquid polish, this one includes liquid paraffin.

INGREDIENTS

50g/2oz/½ cup beeswax

30ml/2 tbsp carnauba wax

550ml/18fl oz/2½ cups liquid paraffin

1 Using a microwave or bain marie, melt the waxes. Remove from the heat.

2 Stir in the liquid paraffin.

Cream polish

INGREDIENTS

50ml/2fl oz/¼ cup liquid soap

250ml/8fl oz/1 cup water

75g/3oz/5 tbsp beeswax

500ml/17fl oz/generous 2 cups turpentine

50ml/2fl oz/¼ cup pine oil

1 Heat the soap and water. In a bain marie, melt the beeswax and add the turpentine and pine oil.

2 When each mix is cool, mix together.

Leather treatment

To waterproof leather, nourish and stop it cracking, prepare the treatment below and, while still warm, apply with a dry cloth, or, brush it on to the leather. Polish with a clean dry cloth.

INGREDIENTS

50g/2oz/½ cup beeswax

50g/2oz/½ cup resin

600ml/1 pint/2½ cups vegetable oil

1 Using a microwave or bain marie, gently melt the beeswax.

2 Add the resin and oil. Stir well to mix.

REMOVING BEESWAX FROM A CARPET

To remove beeswax from carpet and upholstery, take off as much beeswax as possible by hand, then place a piece of kitchen or brown paper over the area. Apply a warm iron, moving over the wax as it soaks into the paper. Apply with care, as some fabrics may be too delicate for this treatment.

BEESWAX AND HONEY SOAP

Containing both beeswax and honey, this soap has an aromatic fragance and a moisturizing texture. Add flowers or herbs if you wish, or oatmeal for an exfoliating effect.

This mixture sets quickly, so any added ingredients, including essential oils for fragrance, colouring and solids, such as pot pourri, herbs or oatmeal, need to be at the ready. The best colourings for soap are from spices and plants, such as turmeric if you want a yellow colour. Experiment with moulds; there are many things around the house that can be used to make interesting soap bars, such as plastic pastry cutters, small bowls or cups. Muffin moulds can make great soap-on-ropes if a looped piece of cord is held upright in the centre of the mould while the liquid is poured around it.

INGREDIENTS
25g/1oz/¼ cup beeswax
50g/2oz/1 cup lye
250ml/8fl oz/1 cup cold water
450ml/¾ pint/scant 2 cups olive oil
25ml/1½ tbsp honey

1 Assemble all the ingredients. Place the beeswax in a heatproof bowl, then melt in a bain marie or microwave.

2 Heat the lye with the water in a pan. Add the olive oil, gently heat, then add to the beeswax. Stir until the mixture is blended and the water has evaporated.

3 Pour the mixture into plastic moulds and cover with greaseproof paper. Leave aside to cool for 48 hours. After cooling, place the moulds in the freezer for about 2 hours. This makes it easier to remove the soap from the moulds.

COLD PROCESS CANDLES

For a speedy sophisticated candle, ready-prepared beeswax sheets are simply rolled up with a wick in the middle to produce a fine candle that burns with a delicate aroma.

INGREDIENTS

sheets of beeswax

cotton wick

1 For a tapered candle, warm some sheets of beeswax with a hairdryer to keep them malleable. The short side of the sheet will determine the height of the candle. Using a craft knife, cut a narrow triangular segment off the longest side.

2▲ Cut a wick that will extend about 2cm/¾in above the height of the candle. Press the wick along the shorter side and roll up. Check that the wick is being held closely from the first turn.

3➤ When you have finished rolling the wax, press the edge into the candle to give a smooth finish. Trim the wick, then wrap a tiny piece of wax around it so that it is primed and ready for burning.

Above: Using sheets of beeswax, you can make candles of the length and width that you prefer.

HOT PROCESS CANDLES

It's fun to make candles at home. You can make basic, traditional dipped candles or use moulds lined with shells or dried herbs to create more stylish candles.

INGREDIENTS

450g/1lb beeswax

colouring (wax crayon or pigment)

25ml/1½ tbsp essential oil (optional)

1 Melt the wax in a bain marie or microwave; you can put the wax in a can and stand it in a saucepan of water. Heat the water to melt the wax, stirring occasionally. Test the temperature of the water with a thermometer. When the temperature is approximately 71°C/160°F, turn down the heat. Stir to avoid air bubbles in the wax.

2 To colour the wax, add small pieces of solid dye, stirring well so that the wax and dye are well blended. Take care not to add too much dye because the colour is very intense. If you wish to add fragrance, add the essential oil of your choice. Stir for 2 minutes to mix thoroughly.

3 Check that the temperature has not dropped; if it has bring it back to 71°C/160°F. Prime the wick by dipping it in the melted wax until it is sealed. Leave to cool, then hang them over a rail. Repeat the dipping and drying processes until the candles are the size you require; this will take 15–30 dips.

4 To give the candles a smooth outer surface, increase the heat of the wax to 82°C/180°F, then dip the candles in the wax for about 3 seconds and leave to cool. When they are cool, trim the bases with a knife until they are flat. Leave the finished candles to cool for at least 1 hour before burning.

HONEYED WOODEN FRESHENER BALLS

Wooden balls scented with honey or beeswax provide instant fragrance. Place them in wardrobes or drawers. The scent will last for several weeks and can be easily revitalized.

INGREDIENTS

100ml/3½fl oz/scant ½ cup
  honey or beeswax
10 drops vanilla extract
4 drops almond extract
1 resealable plastic bag (20 x 20cm/8 x 8in)
10 natural wooden balls

1 In a bowl, gently mix the honey or beeswax with the vanilla and the almond extract and transfer the mixture to a plastic bag.

2 Add the wooden balls to the bag and shake well, making sure all the balls are coated with the mix, then leave for about 1 hour to marinate.

3 Remove the wooden balls from the bag. Using kitchen paper, wipe away the excess honey mixture and transfer to a polishing cloth.

4 Polish the balls well before use.

5 Once polished, the balls are ready to use.

TIP

To revitalize the wooden balls when the scent starts to fade, simply repeat the process. This can be done again and again as required.

GARDENER'S BARRIER CREAM

Working in the garden can be hard on the hands but this cream will protect them from harsh weather and the cold. Beeswax is a good emollient as well as a barrier.

HEALING PROPERTIES

Although it is advisable to wear gloves when gardening, some jobs in the garden require a finer touch and this is when hands can suffer from weather conditions, the cold and the various minor grazes and scratches that are inevitable when you are digging and pruning.

When applied before gardening, this barrier cream will protect the hands and soothe any cuts or scratches sustained.

The ingredients are all designed to keep the hands in the best condition possible. Beeswax is a superior barrier because it seals in moisture. Camomile oil is very soothing and is good for chilblains. Geranium oil helps to heal wounds and scratches quickly, as well as controlling inflammation and improving circulation and skin tone. Lemon oil softens skin that has hardened, while tea tree oil is the natural choice for a gardener because of its antiseptic properties.

INGREDIENTS

25g/1oz each beeswax and lanolin

75ml/5 tbsp almond oil

50ml/3½ tbsp water

10 drops camomile essential oil

5 drops each geranium, lemon and tea
   tree essential oils

1 Slowly melt the beeswax and lanolin in a bain marie or microwave. Whisk and gradually add the almond oil.

2 Still whisking, add the water a few drops at a time. The mixture will become very thick and creamy.

3 Stir in all the essential oils, then decant to a small jar or lidded container. When packed into a rustic box with some honey soap, a nailbrush, a towel and a pumice stone, the gardener will have everything he or she needs to take care of their hands.

WAX CRAYONS

Crayons made with beeswax are sturdy and easy for children to handle and use for drawing and colouring activities. The use of beeswax allows the pigment to shine through.

INGREDIENTS

2 parts beeswax

1 part talc

artist's pigment or food colouring

aluminium foil, rolled up for moulds, one end
  twisted to seal

oil, for brushing

1 Melt the beeswax either in a microwave or in a bain marie. Once liquified, add the talc and then the colouring bit by bit until it reaches the density of colour required.

2 Very carefully pour the hot mixture into the moulds and leave to set. When the wax is beginning to set but is still malleable, gently shape a point at the end of each crayon. Leave until hard.

HONEY FLY TRAP

This simple device for catching flies has even been used by armies on manoeuvre. It is a fairly unusual use of honey, but needs only basic ingredients that you will have in the home.

INGREDIENTS

a large plastic bottle

knife

100ml/3½fl oz/scant ½ cup each of honey
   and water

strong waterproof adhesive tape

60cm/24in of thin string

1 Dampen the label from the plastic bottle and remove it. Rinse out with water and discard the cap. Use the knife to neatly cut the bottle in half.

2 Add the honey and water to a jug and stir thoroughly.

3 Pour the honey mixture into the bottom half of the bottle. Invert the top half of the bottle into the bottom part of the bottle so that the neck of the bottle faces downwards. To prevent flies drowning, use paper to screen the liquid.

4 Tape the two halves of the bottle together, using a strong waterproof adhesive tape. Wind the tape around twice to ensure that the structure holds together when it is hung up. Replenish the mixture when required.

HANGING TRAP

If you want to hang the trap in the garden so that it does not entice rodents, create a hanger as follows. On opposite sides of the container, make two holes, lace 60cm/24in of string through the holes and tie with a secure knot, then hang it up.

A simpler version of this trap simply requires the string to be dipped into pure honey and pinned up wherever required. The flies will stick to the honey and when covered, the string can bagged for disposal.

HONEY IN THE KITCHEN

The oldest sweetener known to man, honey fell out of favour somewhat when cane and beet sugar came on the scene. In recent years it has made a big comeback, however. This is partly because of growing interest in organic foods and partly because more and more people are discovering the versatility of honey and the subtle variations in flavour offered by the different types. Also, unlike sugar, honey has the property of absorbing moisture, so baked foods will stay fresh and moist longer.

Left: The bee motif is a popular one for kitchen china.

COOKING WITH HONEY

Honey adds delicious sweetness and flavour to sweet and savoury foods and has a great affinity with yogurt and ice cream. Used as a marinade, it imparts a lovely glossy finish.

Honey sees us through the day. Many people wake up to a warm drink of tea with honey, or just honey and lemon juice in hot water. At breakfast, honey not only tops cereals, but is also drizzled on muffins and pancakes or simply spread on toast. Honey is often used to sweeten breads and is good in wholemeal (whole-wheat) rolls and loaves.

In a savoury setting, honey makes a delicious vinaigrette: dissolve a little rosemary, alfalfa or orange blossom honey in freshly squeezed lemon or lime juice, then whisk in a mixture of extra-virgin olive oil and sunflower oil.

Honey can also be used as a glaze on roasted vegetables, giving them a lovely flavour and colour. It is particularly good with pumpkin or butternut squash. Honey roast ham is an old favourite, but honey also goes with lamb chops (try mixing it with soy sauce first) and chicken. You can even use honey with fish: honey and salmon sounds unusual

Left: A crusty loaf and some honey are a perfect combination for breakfast.

but it is a winning combination, and it also tastes great with other fish such as trout or mackerel.

When a touch of sweetness is needed to bring out the flavour of tomatoes in a pasta sauce, honey is ideal. It can be stirred into gravies and casseroles and makes a sweet and glossy glaze for barbecued food.

After exercise, a slice of bread spread with honey is a perfect pick-me-up. A slice of honey cake would also do the trick. Because honey was the foremost sweetener for centuries, there are many recipes for different styles of honey cakes around the world. At bedtime, a spoonful of honey in a glass of warm milk will help to ensure a good night's sleep, since it is a recognized soporific.

Buying honey

There are hundreds of different types of honey. Some of the most popular are discussed in detail elsewhere in this book. Colours and flavours vary, and it is worth experimenting to find the ones you like best. In general, dark honeys have more intense taste than pale ones. They also tend to be higher in antioxidants. If you've always bought honey without thinking about the source, basing your choice on texture (clear or creamed) rather than taste, give your taste buds a treat by sampling a selection. You don't need to buy up the store. Just comparing manuka honey,

Above: The cook has many flavours and textures of honey to choose from.

orange blossom and heather honey will give you a glimpse of how different honeys can be, and you'll begin to appreciate how to match individual honeys to specific foods.

Clear or set?

There is no difference nutritionally or chemically between clear (liquid) honey and set honey. Most honey is syrupy when first removed from the comb. Some types stay that way, but most soon start to granulate, that is, the glucose separates out as crystals. The honey looks solid with white crystals, which gives the honey a pale appearance. The honey will be clear or set, depending on the honey's natural propensities and what the market requires. Creamed or churned honey has been commercially crystallized under controlled conditions. This type of honey may have fine white crystals, like a dusting of caster (superfine) sugar, around the top of the jar. This is perfectly normal. Clear honey is treated to discourage granulation.

Storing honey

Honey should be stored at room temperature in a cool, dry place. It will keep almost indefinitely if it is tightly closed. If moisture is allowed to get in to honey it may ferment eventually.

Honey will granulate over time, becoming more solid, but it can easily be liquefied again. Just heat it gently, by placing the open jar in a bowl of hot water, and stir from time to time. Some sources suggest liquefying the honey in a microwave oven, but if you do this, it is vital to use low to medium heat and to warm the honey in short bursts, so that it does not overheat. This would destroy enzymes in the honey and may caramelize it, spoiling the flavour.

Do not store honey in the refrigerator. The exception is borage or viper's bugloss honey, which becomes chewy and toffee-like when chilled, and which is kept in the refrigerator for that reason.

Baking with honey

Honey is sweeter than sugar, so you need around a third less by volume to achieve the same result. Honey also

MEASURING HONEY

If you are measuring honey by the tablespoon, heat the spoon first and the honey will slide off easily. If measuring in a cup, grease the cup first. For larger amounts, weigh the mixing bowl and note its weight, then pour in honey until it is the required weight.

Above: Honey sticks are slim plastic tubes filled with honey for a handy snack.

contains water, so when baking, you need to reduce the amount of other liquids used by about a fifth. A cake recipe might suggest adding a small amount of extra flour, with a raising agent such as bicarbonate of soda (baking soda), to offset the extra liquid. The bicarbonate of soda also neutralizes honey's natural acidity, and helps to make the mixture rise.

An important attribute of honey is that it is hygroscopic, so not only does it contain water, but it also attracts liquid. This is useful in baking, since it means that cakes keep moist and fresh. Cakes that have been sweetened with honey rather than sugar look good because their surfaces become golden brown on baking. To avoid overbrowning, turn down the oven temperature.

If you are baking and need a mild honey, choose an all-purpose variety like blossom honey or try lavender honey. Generally, clear honey is easy to use for baking, but a creamy honey would work in the same way.

Unlike sugar, which just tastes sweet, honey — especially citrus honey — has a flavour of its own. Specialist honeys, like lime, heather or orange blossom, taste delicious when simply spooned out of the jar. Some of the subtler flavours will be lost if the honey is cooked, so use these products as they are, drizzled over tart fruit, mascarpone, blue cheese, ricotta or thick yogurt.

Use honey in marinades and bastes for barbecued foods. The honey will help to tenderize meats and give them a shiny glaze. However, because honey burns quite quickly, lift the meat out of the marinade and blot it before cooking.

Honey can be used to sweeten sorbets and ice creams, and is good in fruit ices or mixtures flavoured with nuts. However, because honey freezes at a lower temperature than sugar, the texture will be different. When making a sugar syrup as the basis for a water ice, use a mixture of honey and caster sugar. Clear heather honey has the best flavour for making ice cream.

USING HONEY INSTEAD OF SUGAR

To substitute honey for sugar when baking, use 225g/8oz honey for every 200g/7oz/1 cup sugar. Reduce the amount of liquid by 60ml/ 4 tbsp. Beat the mixture well, or dissolve the honey in milk. Reduce the oven temperature: if a cake would normally be baked at 180°C/350°F/Gas 4, lower the temperature to 170°C/325°F/Gas 3.

HONEY SMOOTHIES

Easy to prepare and even easier to drink, these energy-packed smoothies make a great start to the day. Honey and fruits provide the perfect fuel to keep your energy levels up.

Mango and honey smoothie

Mango adds a delicious, aromatic flavour to this energy-boosting smoothie. The addition of wheat bran adds more vitamins and minerals, making this an extra healthy drink.

INGREDIENTS

Makes 2 glasses

½ mango
1 banana
1 large orange
30ml/2 tbsp wheat bran
15ml/1 tbsp sesame seeds
10–15ml/2–3 tsp honey

1 Using a small, sharp knife, cut into the mango, carefully remove the skin, then thinly slice the flesh from the stone (pit). Discard any woody flesh near to the stone.

Energy 123Kcal/523kJ; **Protein** 3.4g; **Carbohydrate** 26.9g, of which sugars 23.7g; **Fat** 1g, of which saturates 0.2g; **Cholesterol** 0mg; **Calcium** 40mg; **Fibre** 3.6g; **Sodium** 5mg.

2 Peel the mango and cut in half. Peel the banana then place it in a blender or food processor with the mango. Whizz until smooth.

3 Squeeze the juice from the orange and add to the blender with the bran, sesame seeds and honey. Whizz until smooth, then pour into two glasses.

Raspberry and oatmeal honey smoothie

Oatmeal and honey give substance and a little sweetness to this smoothie. Make it ahead so the oats are easier to digest.

INGREDIENTS

Makes 1 large glass

25ml/1½ tbsp medium oatmeal
150g/5oz/scant 1 cup raspberries
5–10ml/1–2 tsp honey
45ml/3 tbsp natural (plain) yogurt

1 Spoon the oatmeal into a heatproof bowl. Pour in 120ml/4fl oz/½ cup boiling water and stand for 10 minutes.

2 Put the oats in a blender or food processor and add most of the raspberries, the honey and 30ml/2 tbsp of the yogurt.

3 Process until smooth and thick. Pour into a glass, and add the remaining yogurt and reserved raspberries.

Energy 171Kcal/728kJ; **Protein** 7.2g; **Carbohydrate** 31.1g, of which sugars 12.9g; **Fat** 3g, of which saturates 0.3g; **Cholesterol** 1mg; **Calcium** 131mg; **Fibre** 4.8g; **Sodium** 50mg.

Honey and strawberry smoothie

This energizing blend is full of goodness. It contains honey for energy and tofu, which is full of minerals and nutrients, as well as vitamin-rich strawberries.

INGREDIENTS

Makes 2 glasses

250g/9oz firm tofu
200g/7oz/1¾ cups strawberries
45ml/3 tbsp pumpkin or sunflower seeds,
 plus extra for sprinkling
juice of 2 large oranges
juice of 1 lemon
30–45ml/2–3 tbsp honey

1 Chop the tofu, then hull and chop the strawberries. Reserve four strawberries.

2 Put all the ingredients except the honey into a food processor or blender and blend until completely smooth, scraping the mixture down the sides of the bowl.

3 Add the honey and process again until the mixture is thoroughly blended.

4 Divide the honey and strawberry smoothie between two large glasses.

5 Top each glass with a few of the reserved strawberries and sprinkle with the extra pumpkin or sunflower seeds. Do not store the smoothie – drink it immediately.

Energy 310Kcal/1296kJ; **Protein** 15.7g; **Carbohydrate** 29.6g, of which sugars 22.6g; **Fat** 16.1g, of which saturates 1.7g; **Cholesterol** 0mg; **Calcium** 684mg; **Fibre** 2.5g; **Sodium** 19mg.

Berry honey smoothie

Fresh and frozen cranberries are often in short supply, but dried berries are available all year round and make a tasty dairy-free shake when combined with soya milk and honey.

INGREDIENTS

Makes 1 large glass

25g/1oz/¼ cup dried cranberries
150g/5oz/1¼ cups redcurrants,
 stems removed, plus extra to decorate
10ml/2 tsp clear honey
50ml/2fl oz/¼ cup soya milk
sparkling mineral water

1 Put the cranberries in a small bowl, pour over 90ml/6 tbsp boiling water and leave to stand for 10 minutes.

2 Put the currants in a food processor or blender with the cranberries and soaking water. Blend well until smooth.

3 Add the honey and soya milk and whizz briefly to combine the ingredients.

4 Pour the berry shake into a large glass, then top with a little sparkling mineral water to lighten the drink. Drape the redcurrants over the edge of the glass and serve the smoothie immediately.

Energy 126Kcal/539kJ; **Protein** 3.8g; **Carbohydrate** 27.1g, of which sugars 27.1g; **Fat** 1g, of which saturates 0.1g; **Cholesterol** 0mg; **Calcium** 115mg; **Fibre** 7g; **Sodium** 25mg.

HONEY WITH SHELLFISH

Honey makes a surprisingly good partner for shellfish, adding a subtle touch of sweetness to oysters or scallops. The addition of ingredients such as vinegar or soy sauce gives piquancy.

Warm scallop and honey salad
INGREDIENTS

Serves 4

8 large fresh scallops, each cut into three
15ml/1 tbsp olive oil
15g/½oz/1 tbsp butter
120ml/4fl oz/½ cup dry white wine
300g/11oz/2¾ cups dried conchiglie,
    cooked and drained
90g/3½oz rocket (arugula) leaves,
    stalks trimmed
salt and ground black pepper

For the vinaigrette

60ml/4 tbsp extra virgin olive oil
15ml/1 tbsp balsamic vinegar
1–2 fresh red chillies, seeded and chopped
1 garlic clove, crushed
5–10ml/1–2 tsp clear honey, to taste

1 To make the vinaigrette, put the oil, vinegar and chillies in a jug with the garlic and honey and whisk well.

2 Cook the scallops in the oil and butter until sizzling. Remove with a slotted spoon and keep warm. Add the wine to the liquid remaining in the pan and stir over high heat until reduced to a few tablespoons. Remove from the heat and keep warm.

3 Mix the pasta, rocket, scallops, the reduced cooking juices and the vinaigrette and toss well. Serve.

Energy 535 Kcal/2,252kJ; **Protein** 22.8g; **Carbohydrate** 67.1g, of which sugars 3.4g; **Fat** 19.3g of which saturates 4.4g; **Cholesterol** 32mg; **Calcium** 78mg; **Fibre** 3g; **Sodium** 154mg.

Grilled oysters with heather honey
INGREDIENTS

Serves 4

1 bunch spring onions (scallions)
20ml/4 tsp heather honey
10ml/2 tsp soy sauce
16 fresh oysters

1 Preheat the grill (broiler) to medium. Mix the honey and soy sauce in a small bowl. Finely chop the spring onions and remove any coarse outer leaves. Add to the bowl and mix well.

Energy 81Kcal/343kJ; **Protein** 9.2g; **Carbohydrate** 9.1g, of which sugars 6.9g; **Fat** 1.2g, of which saturates 0.2g; **Cholesterol** 46mg; **Calcium** 121mg; **Fibre** 0.3g; **Sodium** 588mg.

2 Open the oysters and catch the liquid in a bowl. Leave the oysters attached to one side of the shell. Strain the liquid to remove any shell, and set aside.

3 Place a teaspoon of the honey and spring onion mixture on each oyster.

4 Place under the preheated grill for 5 minutes. Take care when removing the oysters as the shells retain the heat. Reserve the sauce from the oyster shells.

5 Allow the oysters to cool slightly before serving with bread to soak up the juices. Tip them into your mouth or lift them out with a spoon or fork.

HONEY WITH FISH

These two salmon recipes are both enhanced by a touch of honey, imparting a delicious counterpoint to coconut and lime, or a delicious sweet-and-sour flavour.

Salmon kebabs with honey

INGREDIENTS

Serves 4

450g/1lb salmon fillet, skinned

1 small fresh coconut

2 limes

12 scallops

45ml/3 tbsp freshly squeezed lime juice

30ml/2 tbsp soy sauce

30ml/2 tbsp clear honey

15ml/1 tbsp soft light brown sugar

ground black pepper

1 Using a sharp knife, cut the salmon into bitesize chunks and place these in a shallow bowl.

2 Halve the coconut and pour the milk into a jug (pitcher). Using a small, sharp knife, remove the coconut flesh from the inside of the shell and cut it into chunks, making them about the same size as the salmon.

3 Cut the limes into six slices. Discard a thin piece from each end of the limes. Thread the coconut, salmon, scallops and lime alternately on to six skewers.

4 Add the lime juice, soy sauce, honey and sugar to the reserved coconut milk for the marinade. Mix and add ground black pepper. You will probably not need salt because the soy sauce is salty.

5 Place the prepared kebabs in a single layer in a shallow non-metallic dish. Pour the marinade over. Cover and chill for at least 3 hours.

6 Preheat the barbecue or the grill (broiler) to high. Remove the kebabs from the marinade and grill (broil) for about 4 minutes on each side, turning once and basting occasionally with the marinade.

Energy 441Kcal/1,837kJ; **Protein** 34.4g; **Carbohydrate** 9.7g, of which sugars 7.3g; **Fat** 29.7g, of which saturates 16g; **Cholesterol** 80mg; **Calcium** 53mg; **Fibre** 3.4g; **Sodium** 637mg.

Honeyed salmon and pineapple

INGREDIENTS

Serves 4

grated rind and juice of 2 limes

15ml/1 tbsp olive oil

1 garlic clove, crushed

30ml/2 tbsp clear honey

15ml/1 tbsp soy sauce

4 salmon fillets, about 200g/7oz each

30ml/2 tbsp sesame seeds

1 small pineapple, skin removed, and sliced

fresh chives, to garnish

1 Mix the lime rind and juice, olive oil, garlic, honey and soy sauce. Pour over the salmon and chill. Preheat the grill (broiler) to high. Sprinkle the sesame seeds over a piece of foil and grill (broil) until golden brown. Set aside.

2 Remove the salmon from the marinade and top with the pineapple rings. Grill for 10 minutes, sprinkle with sesame seeds and garnish with the chives. Serve immediately.

Energy 509Kcal/2,123kJ; **Protein** 39g; **Carbohydrate** 18.7g, of which sugars 18.4g; **Fat** 31.4g, of which saturates 5.4g; **Cholesterol** 100mg; **Calcium** 128mg; **Fibre** 2.1g; **Sodium** 415mg.

HONEY WITH CHICKEN AND DUCK

Honey is a successful ingredient in marinades and glazes for poultry, imparting a glossy finish and a delicious caramelized flavour to the meat.

Chicken satay with honey marinade
INGREDIENTS
Serves 4

4 skinless, boneless chicken breast portions

For the satay sauce
90ml/6 tbsp crunchy peanut butter
1 fresh red chilli, seeded and finely chopped
juice of 1 lime
60ml/4 tbsp coconut milk

For the marinade
2 garlic cloves, crushed
2.5cm/1in piece fresh root ginger, grated
10ml/2 tsp Thai fish sauce
30ml/2 tbsp light soy sauce
15ml/1 tbsp clear honey

1 First, make the satay sauce. Process the ingredients until smooth, then check the seasoning and add more salt or lime juice if necessary. Spoon the sauce into a bowl, cover with clear film (plastic wrap) and set aside.

2 Slice each chicken breast into four long strips. Mix the marinade ingredients in a bowl, then add the chicken strips and toss until coated. Cover and leave for 30 minutes in the refrigerator to marinate. Soak 16 wooden sticks in water, to stop them from burning.

3 Preheat the grill (broiler) to high. Drain the wooden sticks or skewers and the chicken. Thread one strip on to each wooden stick. Grill (broil) for 3 minutes on each side, or until the chicken is golden brown and cooked through. Serve with the satay sauce.

Energy 375Kcal/1,564kJ; **Protein** 42.9g; **Carbohydrate** 3.9g, of which sugars 2.4g; **Fat** 20.9g, of which saturates 5.6g; **Cholesterol** 149mg; **Calcium** 27mg; **Fibre** 1.3g; **Sodium** 249mg.

Honey mustard chicken
INGREDIENTS
Serves 4

8 chicken thighs
60ml/4 tbsp wholegrain mustard
60ml/4 tbsp clear honey
salt and ground black pepper

1 Preheat the oven to 190°C/375°F/Gas 5. Put the chicken thighs in a single layer in a roasting pan. Mix the mustard and honey, season and brush over the chicken thighs.

2 Cook in the preheated oven for 25–30 minutes, brushing the chicken with the pan juices occasionally, until cooked through. To check the chicken is cooked through, skewer it with a sharp knife; the juices should run clear. If the juices run pink, cook for longer and check again.

Energy 250Kcal/1,004kJ; **Protein** 21.6g; **Carbohydrate** 12.1g, of which sugars 12.1g; **Fat** 13.1g, of which saturates 3.6g; **Cholesterol** 90mg; **Calcium** 31mg; **Fibre** 0.7g; **Sodium** 340mg.

Roast duck with honey and thyme
INGREDIENTS

Serves 4

1 duck, washed, patted dry and pricked all
    over with a fork
15ml/1 tbsp butter
1 bunch fresh thyme sprigs
4 slices day-old bread, crumbled
45ml/3 tbsp olive oil, plus an extra
    15ml/1 tbsp for roasting
2 garlic cloves, crushed
10ml/2 tsp dried oregano
45ml/3 tbsp blanched almonds
45ml/3 tbsp clear honey

1 Soak a wooden skewer in water for about 30 minutes. Preheat the oven to 230°C/450°F/Gas 8. Place the duck in a roasting pan, reserving the giblets, and smear the breasts in butter. Place a few sprigs of thyme into the body cavity and crumble the remainder of the leaves over the top of the duck.

2 Put the crumbled bread into a dish and pour the oil over it, rubbing the oil into the bread.

3 Toss in the garlic and oregano, and pack the mixture into the cavity of the duck on top of the thyme sprigs. Skewer the legs with the wooden skewer to prevent the filling from oozing out.

4 Sprinkle the giblets and almonds around the duck and drizzle the honey and the reserved oil over the top. Place the duck in the oven and roast for about 55 minutes until the skin is browned and crisp.

5 Serve the duck straight from the oven with the stuffing, slice the breast and accompany the dish with a tomato and cucumber salad.

Energy 776Kcal/3,241kJ; **Protein** 37g; **Carbohydrate** 45.9g, of which sugars 19.6g; **Fat** 50.3g, of which saturates 11.1g; **Cholesterol** 166mg **Calcium** 132mg; **Fibre** 2.5g; **Sodium** 492mg.

Duck with honeyed potatoes
INGREDIENTS

Serves 4

1 duck, washed and patted dry
60ml/4 tbsp light soy sauce
150ml/$\frac{1}{4}$ pint/$\frac{2}{3}$ cup fresh orange juice
3 large floury potatoes, cut into chunks
30ml/2 tbsp clear honey
15ml/1 tbsp sesame seeds
salt and ground black pepper

1 Preheat the oven to 200°C/400°F/Gas 6. Place the duck in a roasting pan. Prick the skin well.

2 Mix the soy sauce and orange juice. Pour over the duck. Cook for 20 minutes.

3 Place the potato chunks in a bowl, stir in the honey and toss to mix well. Remove the duck from the oven and add the potatoes around the duck.

4 Roast for 35 minutes and remove from the oven. Toss the potatoes in the juices and turn the duck over. Return to the oven and cook for another 30 minutes.

5 Remove the duck from the oven and carefully scoop off the excess fat, leaving the juices behind.

6 Sprinkle the sesame seeds over the potatoes, season and turn the duck again, breast side up, and cook for a further 10 minutes. Remove the duck and potatoes from the oven and keep warm. Leave to stand for a few minutes.

7 Pour off the excess fat and simmer the juices on the hob (stovetop) for a few minutes. Serve the juices with the carved duck and potatoes.

Energy 806Kcal/3,341kJ; **Protein** 20.8g; **Carbohydrate** 32.3g, of which sugars 6.4g; **Fat** 66.8g, of which saturates 17.9g; **Cholesterol** 160mg; **Calcium** 53mg; **Fibre** 2.1g; **Sodium** 403mg.

HONEY WITH MEAT

Honey enhances any meat and robustly stands up to spices, herbs and chillies. Lamb, pork and beef dishes all benefit from the addition of honey.

Minted lamb with honey
INGREDIENTS

Serves 2

30ml/2 tbsp olive oil

15ml/1 tbsp lemon juice

30ml/2 tbsp chopped fresh mint

4 lamb chops or steaks

250g/9oz/2 cups leeks, thinly sliced

1 garlic clove, finely chopped

45ml/3 tbsp double (heavy) cream

15ml/1 tbsp clear honey

Lamb with honey and prunes
INGREDIENTS

Serves 6

130g/4½oz/generous ½ cup pitted prunes

350ml/12fl oz/1½ cups hot tea

1kg/2¼lb stewing lamb, cut into chunks

1 onion, chopped

75–90ml/5–6 tbsp chopped fresh parsley

2.5ml/½ tsp ground ginger

2.5ml/½ tsp curry powder

pinch of grated fresh nutmeg

10ml/2 tsp ground cinnamon

1.5ml/¼ tsp saffron threads

75–120ml/5–9 tbsp honey, to taste

250ml/8fl oz/1 cup beef or lamb stock

115g/4oz/1 cup blanched almonds, toasted

30ml/2 tbsp chopped fresh coriander
(cilantro) leaves

3 hard-boiled eggs, cut into wedges

salt and ground black pepper

1 Preheat the oven to 180°C/350°F/ Gas 4. Put the prunes in a bowl, pour over the hot tea and leave to soak up the tea and plump up.

2 Meanwhile, put the lamb into a roasting pan with the onion, parsley, ginger, curry powder, nutmeg, cinnamon, the salt and a large pinch of ground black pepper. Cover the roasting pan and cook in the preheated oven for about 2 hours, or until the meat is just tender.

3 Drain the prunes and add their liquid to the lamb. Combine the saffron and 30ml/2 tbsp hot water and add to the pan with the honey and stock. Bake, uncovered, for 30 minutes, turning occasionally. Add the prunes and serve with the almonds, coriander and egg.

Energy 618Kcal/2,564kJ; **Protein** 42.7g; **Carbohydrate** 0.8g, of which sugars 0.1g; **Fat** 49.3g, of which saturates 21.2g; **Cholesterol** 183mg; **Calcium** 16mg; **Fibre** 0.2g; **Sodium** 150mg.

1 In a shallow container, mix 15ml/ 1 tbsp of the oil with the lemon juice and 15ml/1 tbsp of the mint. Season. Add the lamb and turn in the mint mixture. Leave in the refrigerator for 30 minutes. Turn the lamb twice.

2 Fry the lamb in the remaining oil. Cook over medium heat for 6–8 minutes each side or until browned. Remove from the pan and keep warm.

3 Drain off most of the excess fat from the pan. Add the leeks and garlic, and scrape up any sediment from the base of the pan. Cover and cook over medium heat for 5 minutes, stirring occasionally, until the leeks are soft.

4 Stir in the remaining mint, cream and honey and heat gently until bubbling. Adjust the seasoning if necessary. Serve the leeks in the sauce with the lamb.

Energy 521Kcal/2,166kJ; **Protein** 31.8g; **Carbohydrate** 7.9g, of which sugars 7g; **Fat** 40.5g, of which saturates 17g; **Cholesterol** 145mg; **Calcium** 54mg; **Fibre** 2.8g; **Sodium** 137mg.

Sweet-and-sour pork with honey

INGREDIENTS

Serves 4

30ml/2 tbsp dark soy sauce

15ml/1 tbsp clear honey

400g/14oz pork fillet (tenderloin)

6 shallots, very thinly sliced lengthways

1 lemon grass stalk, thinly sliced

5 kaffir lime leaves, thinly sliced

5cm/2in piece fresh root ginger, sliced

½ fresh long red chilli, seeded and sliced

bunch fresh coriander (cilantro), chopped

For the dressing

30ml/2 tbsp palm sugar

30ml/2 tbsp Thai fish sauce

juice of 2 limes

20ml/4 tsp thick tamarind juice, made by
    mixing tamarind paste with warm water

1 Preheat the grill (broiler). Put the soy sauce and the honey in a small bowl and mix well.

2 Using a sharp knife, cut the pork fillet lengthways into quarters to make four long, thick strips. Place them in a grill (broiling) pan. Brush with the soy sauce and honey mixture, then grill (broil) for about 10–15 minutes, until cooked through. Turn the strips over often and baste with the honey mixture.

3 Transfer the cooked pork strips to a board. Slice the meat across the grain, then shred it with a fork. Place in a large bowl and add the shallot slices, lemon grass, kaffir lime leaves, ginger, chilli and chopped coriander.

4 Make the dressing. Place the sugar, fish sauce, lime juice and tamarind juice in a bowl. Whisk until the sugar has completely dissolved. Pour the dressing over the pork mixture and toss well to mix, then serve.

Energy 170Kcal/718kJ; **Protein** 22g; **Carbohydrate**, 12.2gof which sugars 12.1g; **Fat** 4g, of which saturates 1.4g; **Cholesterol** 63mg; **Calcium** 16mg; **Fibre** 0.2g; **Sodium** 873mg.

Chilli and honey-cured beef

INGREDIENTS

Serves 4

450g/1lb beef sirloin

2 lemon grass stalks, trimmed and chopped

2 garlic cloves, chopped

2 dried Serrano chillies, seeded and chopped

30–45ml/2–3 tbsp honey

15ml/1 tbsp *nuoc mam* (fish sauce)

30ml/2 tbsp soy sauce

rice wrappers, fresh herbs
    and dipping sauce, to serve (optional)

1 Trim the beef and cut it against the grain into thin, rectangular slices.

2 Using a mortar and pestle, grind the lemon grass, garlic and chillies to a paste. Stir in the honey, nuoc mam and soy sauce. Put the beef into a bowl, tip in the paste and rub it into the meat.

3 Arrange the meat on a rack and put it in the refrigerator, uncovered, for 2 days.

4 Cook the beef on the barbecue and serve as a snack on its own or with rice wrappers, herbs and a dipping sauce.

Energy 138Kcal/581kJ; **Protein** 18g; **Carbohydrate** 9g, of which sugars 8g; **Fat** 3g, of which saturates 2g; **Cholesterol** 38mg; **Calcium** 7mg; **Fibre** 0.1g; **Sodium** 40mg.

HONEY WITH VEGETABLES

Honey brings out the maximum flavour in a range of vegetable dishes, as well as adding a tantalizing hint of sweetness. It also makes a delicious glaze for vegetables.

Honeyed red cabbage with spices
INGREDIENTS

Serves 4

3 thick, rindless bacon rashers, diced

1 large onion, chopped

1 large red cabbage, evenly shredded

3 garlic cloves, crushed

15–25ml/1–1½ tbsp caraway
    seeds

120ml/4fl oz/½ cup water

2 firm, ripe pears, peeled,
    cored and chopped

juice of 1 lemon

475ml/16fl oz/2 cups red wine

45ml/3 tbsp red wine vinegar

150g/5oz/scant ¾ cup clear honey

salt and freshly ground black pepper

caraway seeds and snipped fresh chives,
    to garnish

1 Dry fry the bacon over low heat for 5–10 minutes, or until golden brown. Stir in the onion and cook for 5 minutes or until pale golden.

2 Stir the cabbage, garlic, caraway seeds and the water into the pan. Cover and cook for 8–10 minutes. Season, then add the pears, lemon juice, red wine and vinegar. Cover and cook for 15 minutes. Stir in the honey.

3 If there is too much cooking liquid, remove the lid and allow it to reduce. The pears will have broken up in the pot, and the quantity reduced by one-third. Adjust the seasoning to taste and serve sprinkled with caraway seeds and snipped fresh chives.

Energy 112Kcal/469kJ; **Protein** 2g; **Carbohydrate** 17.1g, of which sugars 15.5g; **Fat** 2.4g, of which saturates 1.3g; **Cholesterol** 5mg; **Calcium** 55mg; **Fibre** 3.1g; **Sodium** 25mg.

Honeyed vegetables
INGREDIENTS

Serves 6

250g/9oz carrots, peeled and sliced

1 sweet potato, peeled and cut into chunks

1 potato, peeled and cut into chunks

pinch of sugar

30ml/2 tbsp vegetable oil

1 onion, chopped

10 pitted prunes, halved or quartered

30–45ml/2–3 tbsp currants

5 dried apricots, roughly chopped

30ml/2 tbsp honey

5–10ml/1–2 tsp chopped fresh root ginger

1 cinnamon stick

1 Preheat the oven to 160°C/325°F/ Gas 3. Put the carrots, sweet potato and potato into a pan of sugared and salted boiling water and cook until almost tender. Drain, reserving the cooking liquid, and set aside.

2 Heat the oil in a flameproof casserole, add the onion and fry until softened. Add the cooked vegetables and enough of the cooking liquid to cover the vegetables completely, then add the remaining ingredients.

3 Cover and cook in the oven for 40 minutes. Near the end of cooking time, check the liquid. If there is too much liquid, remove the lid for the last 15 minutes.

Energy 143Kcal/601kJ; **Protein** 1.9g; **Carbohydrate** 26.8g, of which sugars 15.9g; **Fat** 3.9g, of which saturates 2.3g; **Cholesterol** 9mg; **Calcium** 36mg; **Fibre** 2.9g; **Sodium** 55mg.

Honeyed artichoke hearts

Globe artichokes are cooked in a honey dressing with ginger and preserved lemons. This dish makes a good accompaniment to barbecued meat.

INGREDIENTS

Serves 4

30–45ml/2–3 tbsp olive oil

2 garlic cloves, crushed

scant 5ml/1 tsp ground ginger

pinch of saffron threads

juice of $\frac{1}{2}$ lemon

15–30ml/1–2 tbsp honey

peel of 1 preserved lemon, finely sliced

8 artichoke hearts, quartered

150ml/$\frac{1}{4}$ pint/$\frac{2}{3}$ cup water

salt

Honey and sour cream gherkins

This salad has Russian origins, and it is traditionally served with a selection of hors d'oeuvres, called zakouski. The honey marries perfectly with the sour cream to give a delightful sweet and sour flavour to the dish. It could act as a perfect foil to grilled or roast pork.

INGREDIENTS

Serves 4

4 large pickled gherkins

60ml/4 tbsp sour cream

15g/$\frac{1}{2}$oz/1 tbsp butter

60ml/4 tbsp clear honey

1 Slice the gherkins lengthways into quarters. Whisk the sour cream until light and foamy, then spoon on to four individual serving plates.

2 Put the butter in a frying pan and heat until melted. Add the gherkin slices and turn in the butter until warmed, then pile on top of the sour cream.

3 Pour the honey into the pan and stir well until all the butter and residue on the bottom of the pan are thoroughly incorporated. Spoon over the gherkins and serve hot.

Energy 106Kcal/441kJ; Protein 0.8g; Carbohydrate 12.6g, of which sugars 12.6g; Fat 6.1g, of which saturates 3.8g; Cholesterol 17mg; Calcium 22mg; Fibre 0.2g; Sodium 32mg.

1 Heat the olive oil in a heavy pan and add the garlic. Before the garlic begins to colour, stir in the ginger, saffron, lemon juice, honey and preserved lemon peel. Add the artichokes and toss them in the spices and honey. Add the water and salt and heat until simmering.

2 Cover the pan and simmer for 10–15 minutes. If the liquid has not reduced, take the lid off the pan and boil for 2 minutes until it is reduced to a coating consistency. Serve warm.

Energy 142Kcal/586kJ; Protein 1.6g; Carbohydrate 4.1g, of which sugars 1.9g; Fat 11.3g, of which saturates 1.6g; Cholesterol 0mg; Calcium 40mg; Fibre 1.6g; Sodium 47mg.

HONEY IN DESSERTS

A more obvious use of honey is to sweeten and flavour fruity desserts and ices. Because honey is sweeter than sugar, around one-third less is needed for desserts.

Raspberry and honey bombe
INGREDIENTS

Serves 4

750ml/1¼ pints/3 cups raspberry sorbet
550ml/18fl oz/2½ cups double (heavy) cream
60ml/4 tbsp clear honey
75ml/5 tbsp whisky
50g/2oz/½ cup medium oatmeal, toasted

1 Stand the sorbet at room temperature for 20 minutes. Chill a 1.5 litre/2½ pint/6¼ cup bombe mould. Pack the sorbet on to the base and sides of the mould. Return to the freezer.

2 Whip the cream with the honey and whisky until softly peaking. Fold in the oatmeal. Spoon into the mould and level the surface. Cover and freeze.

3 To serve, loosen the edges of the mould. Dip the mould into hot water, lift out, hold a plate over the top of the mould, then invert on to the plate. Serve.

Energy 518Kcal/2158kJ; **Protein** 3g; **Carbohydrate** 39.2g, of which sugars 34.6g; **Fat** 37.7g, of which saturates 23g; **Cholesterol** 94mg; **Calcium** 68mg; **Fibre** 2.2g; **Sodium** 22mg.

Poached pears in scented honey
INGREDIENTS

Serves 4

45ml/3 tbsp clear honey
juice of 1 lemon
250ml/8fl oz/1 cup water
pinch of saffron threads
1 cinnamon stick
2–3 dried lavender heads
4 firm pears, peeled, stalk attached

1 Heat the honey and lemon juice in a heavy pan until the honey has dissolved. Add the water, saffron threads, cinnamon stick and the flowers from 1–2 lavender heads. Bring to the boil, reduce the heat, then simmer for 5 minutes.

2 Add the whole pears to the pan and simmer gently for 20 minutes until they are tender. Leave to cool in the syrup and serve at room temperature, decorated with a few lavender flowers.

Energy 283Kcal/1,207kJ; **Protein** 0.8g; **Carbohydrate** 74.3g, of which sugars 74.3g; **Fat** 0.2g, of which saturates 0g; **Cholesterol** 0mg; **Calcium** 38mg; **Fibre** 3.3g; **Sodium** 10mg.

Ricotta honey cakes with fruit sauce
INGREDIENTS

Serves 4

250g/9oz/generous 1 cup ricotta cheese
2 egg whites
60ml/4 tbsp scented honey, plus extra to taste
450g/1lb/4 cups mixed fresh or frozen fruit, such as strawberries, raspberries or cherries

1 Preheat the oven to 180°C/350°F/ Gas 4. Beat the ricotta with the egg whites and honey until smooth. Grease four ramekins. Spoon in the mixture and level the tops. Bake for 20 minutes.

2 For the fruit sauce, reserve some fruit for decoration, put the rest in a pan, with water if the fruit is fresh, and heat until soft. Cool slightly and remove any stones (pits). Press through a sieve, and sweeten with honey. Serve the sauce, warm or cold, with the cakes. Decorate with the reserved berries.

Energy 176Kcal/741kJ; **Protein** 8g; **Carbohydrate** 21g, of which sugars 21g; **Fat** 7g, of which saturates 4g; **Cholesterol** 31mg; **Calcium** 173mg; **Fibre** 1.4g; **Sodium** 100mg.

Crème fraîche and honey ice

This delicately flavoured vanilla ice cream is delicious served with hot apple pie.

INGREDIENTS

Serves 4

4 egg yolks
60ml/4 tbsp clear flower honey
5ml/1 tsp cornflour (cornstarch)
300ml/½ pint/1¼ cups milk
7.5ml/1½ tsp natural vanilla extract
250g/9oz/generous 1 cup crème fraîche
nasturtium or herb flowers, to decorate

1 Whisk the egg yolks, honey and cornflour in a bowl until thick and foamy. Bring the milk to the boil, then pour on to the yolk mixture, whisking.

Energy 386Kcal/1602kJ; **Protein** 6.9g; **Carbohydrate** 16.5g, of which sugars 16.3g; **Fat** 33g, of which saturates 19.5g; **Cholesterol** 277mg; **Calcium** 151mg; **Fibre** 0g; **Sodium** 57mg.

2 Return the mixture to the pan and cook over low heat, stirring all the time until the custard thickens and is smooth. Pour it back into the bowl, then set aside until cool.

3 Stir in the vanilla extract and crème fraîche. Pour into a plastic tub or similar freezerproof container. Freeze for about 6 hours or until firm enough to scoop, beating once or twice with a fork or in a food processor to break up the ice crystals.

Fresh figs baked with honey

Baking fruit with honey is an ancient cooking method.

INGREDIENTS

Serves 4

12 ripe figs
30ml/2 tbsp sugar
3–4 cinnamon sticks
45–60ml/3–4 tbsp clear honey
225g/8oz/1 cup natural (plain) yogurt

1 Preheat the oven to 200°C/400°F/ Gas 6. Wash the figs and pat dry with kitchen paper. Cut a deep cross from the top of each fig to the bottom, keeping the skin at the bottom intact. Fan each fig out to look like a flower, then place upright in a baking tin (pan).

2 Sprinkle the sugar over each fig flower, tuck in the cinnamon sticks and drizzle with the honey. Bake for about 15–20 minutes, until the sugar is slightly caramelized but the honey and figs are still moist. Check to make sure they are not browning too much and if they are, cover them with baking foil for the rest of the cooking time.

3 Remove the cinnamon sticks before serving the figs. Eat warm with yogurt .

Energy 198Kcal/845kJ; **Protein** 2.3g; **Carbohydrate** 48.2g, of which sugars 48.2g; **Fat** 1g, of which saturates 0g; **Cholesterol** 0mg; **Calcium** 155mg; **Fibre** 4.5g; **Sodium** 39mg.

BAKLAVA

Honey is essential for this traditional pastry, which is soaked in a sweet honey and lemon syrup overnight. The result is a sticky, richly delicious mouthful.

INGREDIENTS

Makes 24 pieces

175g/6oz/³⁄₄ cup butter, melted
400g/14oz packet filo pastry, thawed if
    frozen
30ml/2 tbsp lemon juice
60ml/4 tbsp clear honey
50g/2oz/¹⁄₄ cup caster (superfine) sugar
finely grated rind of 1 lemon
10ml/2 tsp cinnamon
200g/7oz/1³⁄₄ cups blanched
    almonds, chopped
200g/7oz/1³⁄₄ cups walnuts, chopped
75g/3oz/³⁄₄ cup pistachios or hazelnuts,
    chopped
chopped pistachios,
    to decorate

For the syrup
350g/12oz/1³⁄₄ cups caster sugar
115g/4oz/¹⁄₂ cup clear honey
600ml/1 pint/2¹⁄₂ cups water
2 strips of lemon rind, thinly pared

1 Preheat the oven to 160°C/325°F/ Gas 3. Brush the base of a shallow 30 x 20cm/12 x 8in loose-bottomed or Swiss roll tin (jelly roll pan) with melted butter. Cut the sheets of filo pastry with a sharp knife to fit the tin exactly.

2 Place one sheet of pastry in the base of the tin, brush with a little melted butter, then repeat until you have used half of the pastry sheets. Set the remaining pastry aside and cover.

3 To make the filling, place the lemon juice, honey and sugar in a pan and heat gently until dissolved. Stir in the lemon rind, cinnamon and nuts. Mix well.

4 Spread half the filling over the pastry, cover with 3 layers of pastry and butter, then spread with the remaining filling.

5 Finish by using up the remaining pastry and butter on top, and brush the top of the pastry liberally with butter.

Energy 282Kcal/1179kJ; **Protein** 4.1g; **Carbohydrate** 27.4g, of which sugars 23.8g; **Fat** 18.1g, of which saturates 4.9g; **Cholesterol** 16mg; **Calcium** 48mg; **Fibre** 1.2g; **Sodium** 64mg.

6 Using a sharp knife, carefully mark the pastry into squares, almost cutting through the filling. Bake in the preheated oven for 1 hour, or until crisp and golden brown.

7 Meanwhile, make the syrup. Place the sugar, honey, water and lemon rind in a pan and stir over low heat until the sugar and honey have dissolved. Bring to the boil, then boil for a further 10 minutes until the mixture has thickened slightly.

8 Take the syrup off the heat and leave to cool slightly. Remove the baklava from the oven. Remove and discard the lemon rind from the syrup, then pour over the pastry. Leave to soak for 6 hours or overnight. Cut into squares and serve, decorated with pistachios.

HONEY SWEETS

Honey is wonderful in home-made sweets. Meltingly good vanilla and honey fudge and honey-flavoured nougat are sure to become favourites.

Nutty honey nougat
INGREDIENTS
Serves 4

225g/8oz/generous 1 cup sugar
225g/8oz/1 cup clear honey
1 large (US extra large) egg white
115g/4oz/1 cup flaked (sliced) almonds, roasted

Vanilla honey fudge
INGREDIENTS
Makes about 60 pieces

175g/6oz/³⁄₄ cup butter
675g/1¹⁄₂lb/3 cups soft light brown sugar
400g/14oz can sweetened condensed milk
60ml/4 tbsp honey
2.5ml/¹⁄₂ tsp vanilla extract

1 Butter a shallow tin (pan). Warm the butter and 150ml/¹⁄₄ pint/²⁄₃ cup water in a heavy pan until the butter melts.

2 Add the sugar and stir over low heat until dissolved. Raise the heat and bring to the boil. Boil until it reaches hard crack stage (168°C/336°F on a sugar thermometer). Test by pouring a small amount into a saucer of cold water to form strands that can be cracked.

3 Remove the pan from the heat and add the condensed milk and honey. Return to the heat, stirring, for a few minutes. Remove from the heat, add the vanilla extract, and beat with a wooden spoon until the mixture is glossy. Pour into the tin, then leave to cool.

4 Cut into cubes and store in an airtight tin. Place in petits fours cases to serve.

Energy 103Kcal/435kJ; **Protein** 0.7g; **Carbohydrate** 19.4g, of which sugars 19.4g; **Fat** 3.1g, of which saturates 1.9g; **Cholesterol** 9mg; **Calcium** 28mg; **Fibre** 0g; **Sodium** 28mg.

1 Line a 17.5cm/7in square cake tin (pan) with rice paper. Place the sugar, honey and 60ml/4 tbsp water in a large, heavy pan and heat gently, stirring often, until the sugar has dissolved.

2 Bring to the boil and boil to the soft crack stage (when the syrup forms hard but not brittle threads in cold water) or 151°C/304°F on a sugar thermometer. Whisk the egg white until stiff, then drizzle in the syrup while whisking.

3 Stir in the nuts and pour the mixture into the tin. Cool but, before the nougat becomes too hard, cut it into squares.

Energy 392Kcal/1,636kJ; **Protein** 10g; **Carbohydrate** 28.3g, of which sugars 27.8g; **Fat** 27.4g, of which saturates 13g; **Cholesterol** 54mg; **Calcium** 266mg; **Fibre** 1.5g; **Sodium** 161mg.

HONEY IN BAKING

Honey particularly lends itself to aromatically spiced cakes and cookies and is a favourite in any sweet bars and buns. Honey attracts moisture so that baked goods stay moist and fresh.

Spicy honey cake

INGREDIENTS

Serves 8

175g/6oz/1½ cups plain (all-purpose) flour
75g/3oz/⅓ cup caster (superfine) sugar
2.5ml/½ tsp ground ginger
2.5–5ml/½–1 tsp ground cinnamon
5ml/1 tsp mixed (apple pie) spice
5ml/1 tsp bicarbonate of soda
   (baking soda)
225g/8oz/1 cup clear honey
60ml/4 tbsp vegetable or olive oil
grated rind of 1 orange
2 eggs
75ml/5 tbsp orange juice
10ml/2 tsp chopped fresh root ginger

1 Preheat the oven to 180°C/350°F/ Gas 4. Line a rectangular baking tin (pan), measuring 25 x 20 x 5cm/ 10 x 8 x 2in, with a sheet of baking parchment. In a large mixing bowl, stir together the flour, sugar, ginger, cinnamon, mixed spice and bicarbonate of soda.

2 Make a well in the centre of the flour mixture and pour in the honey, oil, orange rind and eggs. Beat until smooth, then add the orange juice and ginger.

3 Pour the cake mixture into the prepared tin, then bake for about 50 minutes, or until firm to the touch.

4 Leave the cake to cool in the tin, then turn out and wrap tightly in foil. Store at room temperature for 2–3 days before serving to allow the flavours of the cake to mature.

Energy 152Kcal/640kJ; **Protein** 1.9g; **Carbohydrate** 23.6g, of which sugars 13g; **Fat** 6.3g, of which saturates 3.8g; **Cholesterol** 26mg; **Calcium** 30mg; **Fibre** 0.4g; **Sodium** 49mg.

Honey cookies

INGREDIENTS

Makes 20

2.5ml/½ tsp bicarbonate of soda
   (baking soda)
grated rind and juice of 1 large orange
150ml/¼ pint/⅔ cup extra virgin olive oil
75g/3oz/6 tbsp caster (superfine) sugar
60ml/4 tbsp brandy
7.5ml/1½ tsp ground cinnamon
400g/14oz/3½ cups self-raising (self-rising)
   flour, sifted with a pinch of salt
225g/8oz/1 cup clear honey
115g/4oz/½ cup caster (superfine) sugar
115g/4oz/1 cup walnuts, chopped,
   to decorate

1 Mix the bicarbonate of soda and orange juice. Beat the oil with the sugar, add the brandy and cinnamon, then add to the orange juice. Add the flour and salt into the mixture, then the orange rind, and knead for 10 minutes.

2 Preheat the oven to 180°C/350°F/ Gas 4. Flour your hands and shape small pieces of dough into ovals and place on baking sheets. Flatten the cookies a little, then bake for 25 minutes. Cool.

3 Bring the honey, sugar and 150ml/ ¼ pint/⅔ cup water to the boil, skim, then simmer for 5 minutes. Immerse the cookies in the syrup for 2 minutes. Sprinkle with the walnuts.

Energy 118Kcal/495kJ; **Protein** 1.3g; **Carbohydrate** 17.3g, of which sugars 10.1g; **Fat 5.3g**, of which saturates 3.2g; **Cholesterol** 26mg; **Calcium** 21mg; **Fibre** 0.3g; **Sodium** 39mg.

Honey and walnut bars

INGREDIENTS

Makes 12–14

175g/6oz/1½ cups plain (all-purpose) flour

30ml/2 tbsp icing (confectioners')
    sugar, sifted

115g/4oz/½ cup unsalted (sweet)
    butter, diced

For the topping

300g/11oz/scant 3 cups walnut halves

2 eggs, beaten

50g/2oz/¼ cup unsalted (sweet)
    butter, melted

50g/2oz/¼ cup light muscovado
    (brown) sugar

90ml/6 tbsp dark clear honey

30ml/2 tbsp single (light) cream

1 Preheat the oven to 190°C/375°F/Gas
5. Grease a 28 x 18cm/11 x 7in tin (pan).

2 Put the flour, icing sugar and butter in
a food processor and process until the
mixture forms crumbs. Using the pulse
button, add 15–30ml/1–2 tbsp water –
enough to make a firm dough.

3 Roll the dough out and line the base
and sides of the tin. Trim and fold the
top edge inwards.

4 Prick the base, line with foil and
baking beans and bake blind for 10
minutes. Remove the foil and beans.
Return to the oven for 5 minutes, until
cooked but not browned. Reduce the
temperature to 180°C/350°F/Gas 4.

5 For the topping, sprinkle the nuts
over the base. Whisk the remaining
ingredients. Pour over the walnuts and
bake for 25 minutes. Leave to cool.

Energy: 333Kcal/1,386kJ; **Protein** 5.4g; **Carbohydrate**
21.4g, of which sugars 11.7g; **Fat** 25.7g, of which
saturates 7.8g; **Cholesterol** 53mg; **Calcium** 49mg;
Fibre 1.1g; **Sodium** 85mg.

Honey and spice cakes

INGREDIENTS

Makes 18

250g/9oz/2 cups plain (all-purpose) flour

5ml/1 tsp ground cinnamon

5ml/1 tsp bicarbonate of soda (baking soda)

125g/4½oz/½ cup butter, softened

125g/4½oz/½ cup soft brown sugar

1 large (US extra large) egg, separated

125g/4½oz clear honey

about 60ml/4 tbsp milk

caster (superfine) sugar, for sprinkling

1 Preheat the oven to 200°C/400°F/
Gas 6. Lightly butter a bun tin (pan)
or line the bun tin with paper cases.

2 Sift the flour into a large mixing
bowl with the cinnamon and the
bicarbonate of soda.

3 Beat the butter with the sugar until
light and fluffy. Beat in the egg yolk,
then gradually add the honey.

4 With a large metal spoon and a
cutting action, fold in the flour
mixture plus sufficient milk to make
a soft mixture that will just drop
off the spoon.

5 In a separate bowl, whisk the egg
white until stiff peaks form. With a large
metal spoon, using a figure-of-eight
movement, fold the egg white
into the cake mixture.

6 Divide the mixture among the paper
cases or distribute the mixture in the
prepared tin. Put into the hot oven and
cook for 15–20 minutes or until risen,
firm and springy to the touch and
golden brown.

7 Sprinkle the tops of the buns lightly
with caster sugar, then leave to cool
completely on a wire rack.

Energy 152Kcal/639kJ; **Protein** 1.9g; **Carbohydrate**
23.6g, of which sugars 13g; **Fat** 6.3g, of which
saturates 3.8g; **Cholesterol** 26mg; **Calcium** 30mg;
Fibre 0.4g; **Sodium** 49mg.

HONEY IN DRESSINGS, RELISHES AND DIPS

Honey is surprisingly delicious in salad dressings, adding a sweet touch that complements many ingredients. Dips and relishes also benefit from the addition of honey.

Honey and mustard dressing
This tangy dressing gives a kick to a tuna, pasta and corn salad.

In a bowl, mix 60ml/4 tbsp extra virgin olive oil, 15ml/1 tbsp balsamic vinegar, 5ml/1 tsp red wine vinegar, and 5ml/1 tsp Dijon mustard with 10ml/2 tsp clear honey. Add to the salad and toss well to mix.

Honey and herb dressing
Mixed herbs, honey, oil and lemon are a perfect foil for a spicy sausage salad.

Mix 30ml/2 tbsp lemon juice, 15ml/1 tbsp clear honey, 90ml/6 tbsp olive oil, 10ml/2 tsp French mustard, 30ml/2 tbsp chopped fresh herbs, such as coriander (cilantro), chives and parsley. Pour over the salad.

Honey and citrus dressing
Orange rind and juice, honey and oil make a light, zesty dressing for chicken.

To 15ml/1 tbsp honey, add the juice and grated rind of 1 orange, segments from 2 limes, 30ml/2 tbsp chopped tarragon and 60ml/4 tbsp olive oil. Mix thoroughly, season to taste and spoon over a chicken salad.

Honey and chipotle relish
This smoky-flavoured relish is great in sandwiches or just served on its own.

Drain 400g/14oz can tomatoes. Discard the juice. In a blender or food processor, mix the tomatoes, 5 chipotle chillies, 3 garlic cloves, 60ml/4 tbsp clear honey, 5ml/1 tsp dried oregano, 5ml/1 tsp American mustard and 150ml/¼ pint/⅔ cup red wine. Process until smooth. Serve with grilled (broiled) or barbecued meats.

Honey, carrot and almond relish
This honeyed relish is a perfect accompaniment to grilled meat.

In a pan, mix 15ml/1 tbsp ground coriander with 500g/1¼lb grated carrots, 50g/2oz shredded root ginger, juice and grated rind of 1 lemon, and 30ml/2 tbsp clear honey with 120ml/4fl oz/½ cup wine vinegar. Bring to the boil, then simmer for 30 minutes until the mixure has thickened, stirring often. Add 50g/2oz/½ cup flaked almonds and serve.

Honey and sesame dip
Sesame, lemon and honey combine with mint to make a sweet and tangy dip.

Beat 15ml/3 tbsp light sesame paste with the juice of 1 lemon. Add 30ml/2 tbsp clear honey and 5–10ml/1–2 tsp dried mint and beat again until the mixture is thick and creamy. Spoon into a small dish and serve at room temperature with lemon wedges for squeezing. This dip is good served with chunks of crusty fresh bread or toasted pitta bread.

HONEY IN MARINADES AND GLAZES

Honey is excellent in savoury dishes, especially in marinades or glazes, when it adds a unique flavour and glossy stickiness to roasted or barbecued meat, poultry and even fruits.

Honey and garlic marinade

Garlic, honey and mushroom soy sauce make a delicious marinade for quails.

In a bowl, beat 150ml/¼ pint/⅔ cup mushroom soy sauce with 45ml/3 tbsp honey. Stir in 8 crushed garlic cloves, 15ml/1 tbsp crushed black peppercorns and 30ml/2 tbsp sesame oil.

Honey and orange marinade

A spicy honey and citrus coating ensures that poultry is moist and succulent.

Combine the juice and grated rind of 2 oranges, 2 crushed garlic cloves, 15ml/1 tbsp chopped root ginger, 45ml/3 tbsp soy sauce, 75ml/5 tbsp honey and 2–3 star anise with 30ml/2 tbsp rice wine.

Honey and ginger marinade

Ginger, sour plum sauce and honey are natural partners in this tasty marinade.

Grind 6 chopped shallots, 4 chopped garlic cloves and 25g/1oz root ginger to a smooth paste. Beat in 30ml/2 tbsp honey, 30ml/2 tbsp each tomato ketchup and sour plum sauce and 15ml/1 tbsp sesame oil.

Honey and spice glaze

Ginger, cinnamon and honey add a fruity, spicy flavour to duck.

Melt 30ml/2 tbsp butter in a pan. Stir in 25g/1oz peeled and grated fresh root ginger and cook for about 1 minute. Add 10ml/2 tsp ground cinnamon, 30ml/2 tbsp clear honey and the juice of 1 lemon. Add 30–45ml/2–3 tbsp water and stir until it bubbles. Simmer until the glaze is reduced and shiny, then pour over roasted meat.

Honey and mustard glaze

When mixed with a tangy mustard, honey peps up chicken wings or legs.

In a small bowl, mix 60ml/4 tbsp clear honey, with 60ml/4 tbsp wholegrain mustard. Beat well and season with salt and ground black pepper to taste. Brush the mixture over chicken portions before grilling (broiling) or barbecuing. Renew the glaze towards the end of the cooking time and make sure that the glaze does not burn.

Honey and soy glaze

Mixed with soy sauce, honey adds a sticky sweet and sour flavour to ribs.

Mix together 75ml/5 tbsp clear honey with 75ml/5 tbsp light soy sauce. Pour or brush over pork spare ribs, turning them several times to ensure they are thoroughly coated. Bake the ribs for 30 minutes at 190°C/375°F/Gas 5, then increase the oven temperature to 220°C/425°F/Gas 7 until there is a thick, sticky glaze on the ribs.

INDEX

Acknowledgements

The author and publishers would like to thank the following individuals and companies for their valuable contributions to this book:

Beekeeper Laurie Wiseman for sharing his expertise.

Rowse Honey Limited for supplying samples from their extensive range of honeys for taste tests and for photography.

The Hive Honey Shop, the largest supplier of English honey and honeybee-related products in the UK, for supplying honey products and artifacts.

The Hive Honey Shop
93 Northcote Road,
London SW11 6PL
Tel. 020 7924 6233
www.thehivehoneyshop.co.uk

Websites and reading

Useful websites
www.honeyassociation.com
www.nhb.org
www.rowsehoney.co.uk

Further reading
Bishop, Holley, *Robbing the Bees* (Simon & Schuster, London, 2005)
Honey, a Book of Recipes (Lorenz Books, London, 1997)
Monk Kidd, Sue, *The Secret Life of Bees* (Headline Book Publishing Ltd, London, 2002)

Picture credits

The publisher would like to thank the following picture libraries for the use of their pictures in the book. Every effort has been made to acknowledge the pictures properly.

l=left, r=right, t=top, b=bottom, bl=bottom left, br=bottom right, m=middle, tr=top right.

Art Archive: 11br; 34.
Bridgeman Art Library: 16.
Corbis: 6m; 11tl; 12t, 12bl &12br; 14; 15b; 17tr; 18t; 19bl; 20bl & 20tr; 21br; 35r; 63tl.
Felicity Forster: 8.
NHPA: 17bl; 18bl.
Nature Picture Library: 13bl; 30tr.
Patricia Ludlow: 10.
Science Photo Library: 13r.